WELCOME

There's no videogame on the planet that's quite like Minecraft. On the surface? It's a fun game where you can build things, do a bit of exploring, and perhaps have the odd fight with a mob you might find on your travels. But start digging deeper, and it soon becomes clear why Minecraft is one of the very few games to ever sell more than 100,000,000 copies worldwide!

You'll find that Minecraft doesn't hold your hand much, though, or offer a great deal of help. That's where we come in! This guide will show you the many secrets and treasures that hide within the game, and it's bursting with tips for Minecraft players of all levels of experience.

Be it working with enchantments, finding secret items, exploring biomes or getting the edge on the many mobs in the game, we've more than got you covered! Just turn the page, and we'll get cracking...

CONTENTS

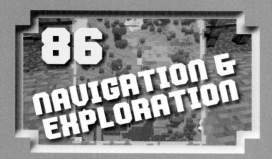

86 NAVIGATION & EXPLORATION

104 NETHER FORTRESSES

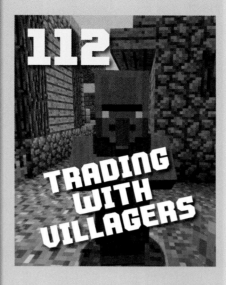

88 VILLAGE SECRETS

140 HOW TO MAKE FIREWORKS

SECRETS FOR GETTING STARTED

Let's Get Going!

Right then! Assuming you've got your copy of Minecraft at the ready, we're kicking off our guide by going through a few secrets to get you started! We're going to explain the importance of many of the game's basics here, and throw in some special secrets about the game that will instantly give you a leg up. In particular, it's worth checking out the special survival tips, which will help keep you safe from the game's assorted creatures!

101 TIPS & SECRETS FROM MINECRAFT EXPERTS

Learning every secret in Minecraft takes forever. That's why we've put together this list of 101 secrets and tips that every expert knows, to turn you from a Minecraft newbie into a pro!

KEEP A LAVA BUCKET HANDY!

USE LAVA AS A HANDY BLOCK INCINERATOR

USE SEA LANTERNS TO LIGHT UNDERWATER

1 Organise your inventory quickbar so that your torches, tools and weapons are easy to reach.

2 Keep lava buckets around as they're 12 times better than a piece of coal for powering a furnace.

3 Iron ingots are very useful – they appear in 27 different crafting recipes, so stock up on them!

4 You can destroy unwanted blocks by throwing them into lava or a fire, or at a cactus.

5 Wood is rare underground. You need it to craft many common items, so if you explore a cave make sure to take some logs with you!

6 Cooked steak and pork chops are common food items that restore a lot of hunger points. Make sure you stock up on them early on!

7 Carry a bed with you so that you can skip nights, but remember that if you die and your last bed is no longer there, you'll be sent back to where you started the map!

8 Don't craft everything straight away. Some resources take up less inventory space than their crafted form (i.e. one bone = two bonemeal). Leaving them uncrafted lets you carry more.

9 Although torches don't work underwater, you can improve light using Jack O'Lanterns, a block of glowstone or sea lanterns.

10 You can skip storms by sleeping, but while you're asleep crops won't grow and smelting pauses!

11 If you have a tame wolf with you, it will run for shelter during a thunderstorm.

12 Mobs wearing helmets or pumpkin heads won't burn in sunlight.

13 If you fall, aim for water, as landing in water prevents you from taking damage when falling.

ABANDONED MINES ARE FULL OF USEFUL WOOD

GOLD HORSE ARMOUR IS STRONGER THAN IRON HORSE ARMOUR

ZOMBIES BURN IN DAYLIGHT

LILY PADS MAKE FOR A USEFUL FOOTBRIDGE

14 When sneaking, it's impossible to fall off cliffs, so if in doubt sneak everywhere!

15 Bunny hopping (sprinting and repeatedly jumping) is quicker than sprinting on its own.

16 Bunny hopping on ice is even faster!

17 Abandoned mineshafts are a good source of emergency wood if you're trapped underground.

18 Stand in a water flow when mining near lava. If you break the wrong block, the water will turn the lava to stone before it damages you.

19 Never dig directly down! There's no way of knowing if you're above a large drop or lava lake.

20 Never dig directly up! Even if you can't see lava or water droplets, there could be a gang of mobs just waiting to drop on you.

21 Try not to dig underwater. It creates a suction current that's hard to swim through and might make you suffocate!

22 Remember that you can sprint straight over one-block gaps without stopping.

23 Gold horse armour is unique in being stronger than its iron counterpart.

24 Zombies burn in daylight, but they can hide in the shade of trees during the day.

25 Axes aren't just useful for chopping trees – they mine any wooden block faster than other tools.

26 Never spend too long underground. When you've collected some resources, turn back and put them in a safe place!

27 You can cast fishing rods onto pressure plates to set them off from a safe distance away!

28 Put lily pads on water to create simple bridges.

29 If you're making fences, remember six Nether bricks will create six Nether brick fences, whereas six sticks will only create two wooden fences.

30 Combining a rod with a carrot on a crafting grid allows you to create a carrot on a stick so you can control saddled pigs.

31 You can use a bucket of water as a portable "elevator". Swimming up and down water flows is quicker than actually building a staircase!

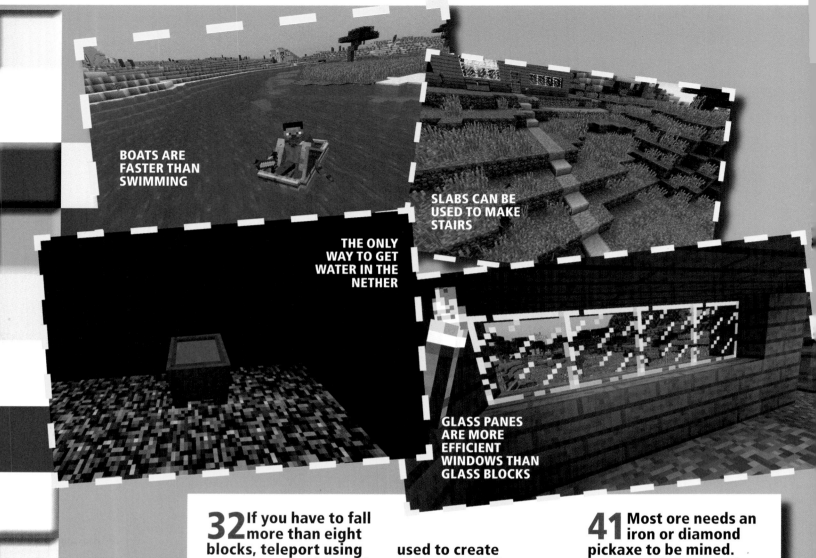

BOATS ARE FASTER THAN SWIMMING

SLABS CAN BE USED TO MAKE STAIRS

THE ONLY WAY TO GET WATER IN THE NETHER

GLASS PANES ARE MORE EFFICIENT WINDOWS THAN GLASS BLOCKS

32 If you have to fall more than eight blocks, teleport using an ender pearl instead and you'll end up taking less damage.

33 Boats are much faster than swimming, so use one whenever you can!

34 Use doors and fence posts to create underwater "airlocks" that let you breathe.

35 When exploring underground, only place torches on the right-hand side of a cave. That way, when you want to find your way back to the surface, all you have to do is make sure the torches are on your left!

36 Half-size blocks like slabs can be used to create staircases with a more gentle incline than actual staircase blocks.

37 Use a crafting table to encase a piece of redstone in wood and you'll create a musical note block.

38 A cauldron can be filled from a water bucket in the Nether.

39 Don't use glass blocks as windows. Six glass blocks make 16 glass panes, so you cover more space using them!

40 You can combine lava and water to create cobblestone, stone or obsidian, depending on which of the two are flowing or still.

41 Most ore needs an iron or diamond pickaxe to be mined. Use any other type of tool and you destroy the block without getting anything from it.

42 If you jump into a hay bale, you only take 20% fall damage.

43 You can often craft four blocks to make nicer-looking blocks: four stone creates stone bricks, and four granite creates polished granite. Try other combinations!

44 If you rename some items, like lapis lazuli, you can't use them as fuel or ingredients.

45 A cauldron has a chance to fill up with water if left in the rain.

46 Sponges can absorb up to 65 blocks of water.

47 Go fishing when it rains and you'll catch items faster.

48 In the latest version of the game, mobs have a 5% chance of spawning left-handed.

49 You can craft mossy stone and bricks by combining vines with cobblestone or stone bricks.

50 Destroying a monster spawner gets you the most experience points in the game (other than killing a boss).

51 Feeding sugar to horses makes them heal faster, grow quicker and tame more easily.

52 On a horse, you can run straight over small gaps and jump over fences and walls.

53 Netherbrick fences don't join up to wooden fences, so you can use a Netherbrick fencepost to create a gate that lets you through but keeps animals penned in.

54 You can feed tame ocelots raw fish to get them to breed. Use clownfish, as these restore very little hunger and have no other use.

55 You can use a fishing rod to hook animals (and mobs) so that you can lead them around.

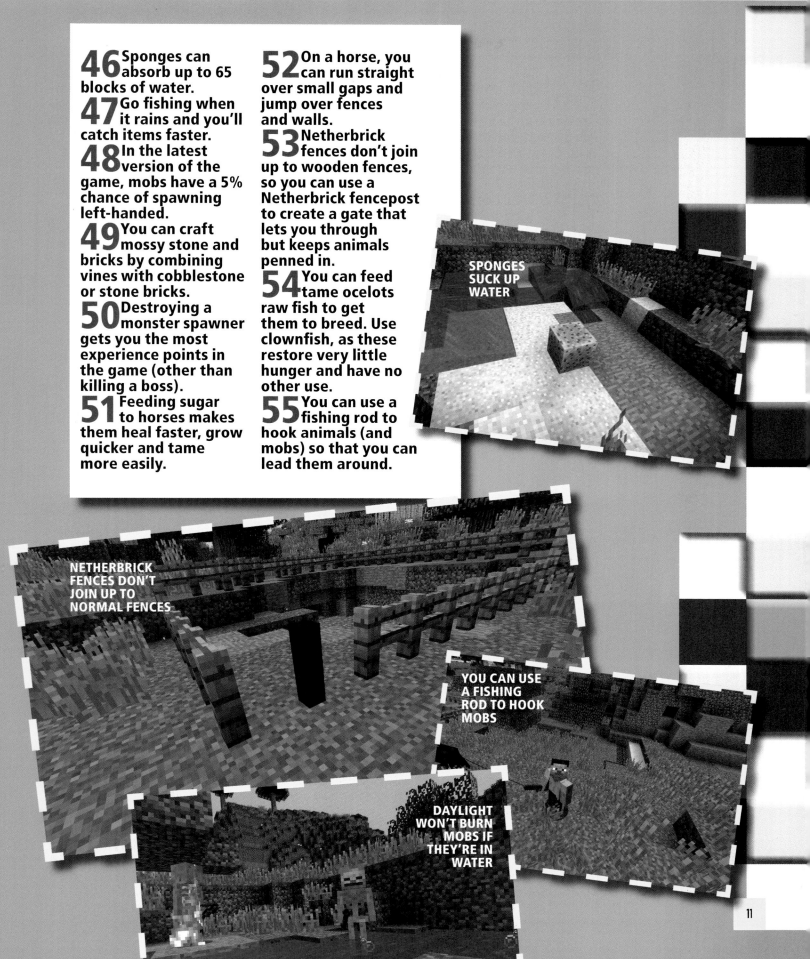

SPONGES SUCK UP WATER

NETHERBRICK FENCES DON'T JOIN UP TO NORMAL FENCES

YOU CAN USE A FISHING ROD TO HOOK MOBS

DAYLIGHT WON'T BURN MOBS IF THEY'RE IN WATER

56 Leads allow you to tie up friendly animals so that they don't wander off. You can create two leads using four string and one slimeball.

57 Witches use a lot of potions. Use a bucket of milk to cure yourself once they've been killed.

58 If you want to keep a zombie or skeleton alive during the day, keep them underwater.

59 Mobs won't cross rails unless they're chasing something, so you can use rails to keep neutral mobs at bay.

60 Harvesting plants and flowers with a tool doesn't do damage to them.

61 The only way to eat a pumpkin is to craft it into pumpkin pie using a pile of sugar and an egg.

62 You can recognise zombie villagers from their faces – they look like green villagers, but not like regular zombies.

63 You can trap endermen by pushing them into a minecart. They can't teleport away!

64 Before you mine diamonds, clear out the blocks around the ore, as you don't want to break the ore block only to find that the diamond falls straight into some hidden lava!

65 Cauldrons can be filled with water and then used to wash the dye off leather clothing, or fill three glass bottles.

66 In the same way that real-life cats always land on their feet, cats (tamed ocelots) in Minecraft don't take fall damage, no matter how high they drop from.

67 If you're low on weapons, remember that lava can damage most enemies. Keep a bucket handy!

68 Fire and lava have no damaging effects on mobs that spawn in the Nether.

ZOMBIE VILLAGERS ALSO WEAR ROBES LIKE VILLAGERS

ENDERMEN CAN'T ESCAPE MINECARTS

CALL A RABBIT TOAST TO GET IT A UNIQUE SKIN

BABY ZOMBIES ARE FASTER AND DON'T BURN

A SHELTER WITH A DOOR CAN EXPAND A VILLAGE

FIRE SPREADS QUICKLY IN JUNGLES

69 Bows are good for killing creepers, but endermen will usually teleport away before an arrow manages to hit them.

70 If you call a rabbit "Toast" with a name tag it will then have a unique black and white skin.

71 You can get lots of experience by fighting blazes. They give 10 experience points per kill, which is at least double than most others.

72 You can heal injured villagers by trading with them or by using a Splash Potion of Healing.

73 Wither skeletons can pick up (and use) discarded bows and swords, so don't drop any nearby!

74 Baby zombies are faster and more powerful than regular zombies, so take them out first!

75 When you fight your first blaze, use a golden apple to boost your stats. After that, you can use blaze rods to make fire resistance potions!

76 If you don't like rain, then good news: you can sleep through storms using a bed, in the same way that you can sleep through nights!

77 You can't eat a glistering melon, but you can use it to create health-restoring potions instead!

78 Lava makes a great (if dangerous) light source. It's one of the few blocks that emits light level 15!

79 You can expand villages by building shelters with doors. Each new door then increases the chances of a new villager spawning.

80 Maps, books and banners can be copied quickly by crafting them with a blank version.

81 You can make it easier to find jungle temples by setting jungles on fire.

82 To play a note block, you can hit it or activate it using a redstone charge. Connect multiple note blocks with redstone to play chords!

83 The sound of a note block changes depending on the material it's placed on.

84 You can force most trees to always grow tall by planting the saplings in holes three blocks deep.

85 Jungle temples are the only place you'll find naturally occurring pistons, levers and dispensers in the Overworld.

86 You can create an infinite water source using just two buckets of water. Simply dig a 2x2 pit and place one water source in each corner.

87 Minecarts travel fastest diagonally. They travel at eight blocks per second when going in a straight line, but 11.3 blocks a second diagonally.

88 Riding in minecarts is 10% slower than sprinting, but you can use the time travelling to craft or reorganise your inventory.

89 On Hard mode, the more full the moon is, the higher the chance a spider will spawn with a random status effect such as speed.

90 Snow golems can be used as an infinite source of snow. Trap them in a pen or room and they'll leave snow wherever they walk, which you can then collect.

91 Beacons can be built overlapping to save resources, as long as the beacon blocks at the top are at least a block apart.

92 If you build a beacon, place it near your home. This will give you the power-up effects where you need them most.

PLANT A TREE THREE BLOCKS DEEP TO FORCE IT TO GROW LARGE WHEN FERTILISED

AN INFINITE WATER SOURCE!

BUILD A BEACON NEAR YOUR HOME

SILVERFISH SUFFOCATE ON SOUL SAND

MINECARTS CAN TRAVEL THROUGH PORTALS

A CREEPER EXPLOSION WON'T HURT YOU IF YOU'RE IN WATER

93 When building redstone circuits, always lay your redstone on easily identifiable blocks such as snow or bricks. This makes sure you don't accidentally destroy them from another angle.

94 Tame wolves are the best way to defeat endermen as they ignore their attacks, even though they do damage!

95 You can build in the End, but leave the entry platform clear. Anything built or placed on it will be erased whenever someone enters the End.

96 Some blocks behave differently in the End: crops won't grow, compasses and clocks don't work, Nether portals will fail to activate, and beds explode when placed.

97 Silverfish and endermites suffocate on soul sand.

98 Minecarts can travel through portals as a shortcut, but make sure you remember to protect their route from mobs!

99 Destroy the pressure plate in desert temples as soon as you find it, otherwise a mob might spawn and set off the TNT!

100 If you repair an enchanted item on a crafting table, you'll lose the enchantment. Use an anvil instead!

101 Hide in water to block out the effects of explosions from TNT going off or exploding creepers.

HEALTH AND HUNGER
EXPLAINED

Health is extremely important in Minecraft, but since low hunger is one of the many things that can lead to low health and ultimately death, make sure you keep a close eye on both of them!

YOUR HEALTH AND HUNGER BARS

EATING FOOD FILLS YOUR HUNGER BAR

TAKING DAMAGE LOWERS YOUR HEALTH BAR

Surviving in Minecraft means keeping track of two things: your health and your hunger. Unless you play in Creative mode (where they don't matter), learning how these parts of the game work allows you to plan ahead, and stay alive long enough to explore and fight!

Health

The health bar is made up of 10 hearts, representing your 20 health points. When you lose a health point, one half of one heart turns black, and if your health bar turns completely black, you'll die.

Health can be lost in lots of different ways: falling from a great height, being hit by a mob or another player, catching on fire, touching lava or a cactus, suffocating when a brick drops on you, drowning in water, getting caught in an explosion or having damaging status effects (like poison.)

You can also starve if you don't keep your hunger bar filled, which we'll talk more about in a moment!

Recovering Health

You can replenish health in several different ways. Some potions and status effects can restore your health either instantly or over time. If your hunger bar has more than 18 full points, your health will regenerate. And if you play on Peaceful mode, the health bar automatically refills regardless of your hunger levels.

Some effects, like Absorption or Health Boost, add health that's temporary, can't be healed and disappears when the status effect runs out. This health usually appears as a separate health bar, with gold hearts above or below the existing one.

16

WHEN YOU WEAR ARMOUR, AN ARMOUR BAR APPEARS

MOBS HAVE HEALTH AND ARMOUR TOO

THE WITHER HAS THE MOST HEALTH IN THE GAME

Armour & Health

You also have an armour bar, which has a varying number of points, depending on the armour you're wearing and what type it is. A full set of the weakest armour (leather) gives you seven armour points, and a full set of the strongest armour (diamond) gives you 20 points.

If you wear armour and take damage, some of the cost will be transferred to the armour rather than your health bar. The strongest armour at full strength will absorb 80% of damage done to the player. Note, though, that some forms of damage won't be affected by armour at all! We'll cover this later.

Mob Health

Like players, mobs also have health, although you can't actually see it. Rabbits (the weakest mob in the game) have three health points, and all of the other passive mobs have 10 health points or fewer, except horses, which can have anywhere between 15 and 30 health points.

Of the hostile mobs, tiny magma cubes and slimes are the weakest with one health point each. Most common mobs – creepers, skeletons and zombies – have 20 health points. Witches have 26, guardians have

30, and elder guardians have 80.

The game's two bosses have the most health: the ender dragon has 200 health points, and the wither has 300!

Like the player, the amount of damage a mob takes can be altered using potions and armour, and can be regenerated with food and potions, so take care what you're chucking about!

SOME ITEMS, LIKE PUFFERFISH, ARE POISONOUS:...

...YOU CAN EAT IT ANYWAY...

...BUT PREPARE FOR THE CONSEQUENCES!

Hunger

As with health, the hunger bar has 20 points represented by 10 icons. Unlike health, which remains constant until the player takes damage, hunger gradually decreases and depends on certain actions the player takes (unless difficulty is set to Peaceful).

When the food bar is full, health regenerates at the speed of one health point per half second, costing one food point for every point healed. If the food bar has 18 points, it will regenerate a health point every four seconds. At 17 points or below, your health won't regenerate.

If the food bar drops below six points, you'll lose the ability to sprint, and if it drops to zero you'll begin losing health. On Easy, you stop losing health at 10 points; on Normal, you stop at one point; and on Hard you can starve to death!

Death

If you lose all of your health, you'll die. This causes two things to happen.

First, you drop all of your items, including armour, and other players (or mobs!) can collect them.

Second, you respawn back in the last bed you slept in or (if that's unavailable) your world's original spawn point (or as close as possible.) If you're quick, you can go and collect your items.

If you play on Hardcore difficulty, death will prevent you from ever editing or interacting with the world you're in, although you can still visit!

PORKCHOPS HAVE VERY HIGH SATURATION

ALL MEAT IS FILLING COOKED, BUT IS IT RIGHT TO EAT MEAT?

IN HARDCORE MODE, HEARTS LOOK DIFFERENT TO REMIND YOU

Hunger Saturation

There's another mechanic in the game related to hunger, and that's called saturation.

Saturation determines how long your hunger bar stays full until it starts to deplete. Generally, complex and rare foods restore a high amount of saturation, and simple, low-quality food only gives a low saturation boost. A golden carrot has the highest saturation, followed by a cooked steak, cooked porkchop and rabbit stew. Clownfish and pufferfish have the lowest saturation.

Saturation is never visible to the player, so you just have to guess whether the food you're eating is keeping your energy high or not.

Health & Hunger Secrets

On Hardcore difficulty, hearts have a different texture to indicate that any death will be permanent!

Every time you die, you see a message explaining how. There are over 40 different messages. How many have you seen?

Sprinting causes your hunger bar to rise faster, so don't do it unless you really need to escape something or have a lot of food on hand!

Hay bales are the only blocks that can be eaten by mobs. They heal up to 10 hearts when fed to a horse, donkey or mule, making them the most efficient way to restore their health.

You can use potions to restore your health, but so can witches!

Stairs aren't just useful for decoration or because they're compact – using them reduces your hunger less than jumping the same distance up or down would.

UNDERSTANDING ORE

As the name suggests, mining is a huge part of Minecraft. The more blocks you find, the more you can build, fight and trade! Here, we'll reveal some secrets you might not know about all the different, valuable ores you can mine in the game.

COAL ORE GENERATES IN HUGE CLUMPS

IRON ORE CAN GENERATE ON OR NEAR THE SURFACE

MESAS CAN HAVE GOLD ORE ON THEIR SURFACE

Coal Ore

When mined with any pickaxe, coal ore drops a piece of coal. It's found at almost every level on a map, and is often easy to see in the exposed stone on mountains and cliffs. The biggest underground coal veins can be up to 64 blocks in size, but are normally around 10-20. Coal is handy for making torches and fuelling furnaces, both of which you'll do a lot!

Iron Ore

A useful all-round resource for making armour and weapons, collecting iron is essential. When mined with a stone pickaxe (or better), iron ore can be collected and smelted into iron ingots. It mostly occurs beneath sea level, but can also occur slightly above it. Typically, iron forms in veins of 4-10 blocks, although two or more veins can generate next to one another.

Gold Ore

Gold is much rarer than most other resources and can only be mined with an iron or diamond pickaxe. Like iron, gold must be smelted into ingots. Gold is softer than iron so has low durability for tools and armour, but enchants more easily and has a faster speed. Gold ore generates in veins of 4-8 blocks and only in the bottom 32 layers of the Overworld, except in mesa biomes.

DIAMOND ORE IS OFTEN FOUND NEAR LAVA

DON'T EVER MISS YOUR CHANCE TO GET EMERALD ORE!

LAPIS LAZULI IS RARE ANYWHERE!

REDSTONE ORE GLOWS IF STRUCK

Diamond Ore

Diamond is a very valuable resource that makes durable tools, powerful weapons, and super strong armour. It can only be found close to the bedrock, in the bottom 15 layers of the Overworld, and is often visible in large caves or near lava. Mining diamond ore with an iron or diamond pickaxe will cause it to drop one diamond, which can then be crafted directly into tools or other items.

Emerald Ore

Emerald is the rarest ore in the game, and is only found in the extreme hills biome at the same depth as gold ore. It doesn't generate in veins, only single blocks at a time. For every block of emerald ore you mine with an iron or diamond pickaxe, you collect one emerald, which is used for trading with villagers.

Lapis Lazuli Ore

Lapis lazuli can be used as blue dye, but it's also an important ingredient for enchanting. The ore can be found underground, and it is most common between levels 13 and 16. You can mine lapis lazuli with a stone, iron or diamond pickaxe.

Redstone Ore

Used for making redstone circuits, redstone dust is Minecraft's version of electrical wires and must be mined from redstone ore. The ore is found in the bottom 16 layers in veins of 4-8 blocks and can be mined with an iron or diamond pickaxe. Redstone dust is also a key ingredient of clocks and compasses.

21

HIDDEN BIOME SECRETS

The different types of terrain you encounter in Minecraft are called biomes. Not only do they all look different, they also have their own features and secrets that are worth learning!

Ice Plains

Ice plains are mostly large and empty, with very few trees, although they're the only place you can find igloos!

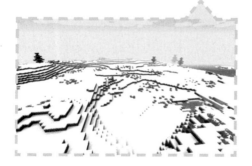

Ice Spikes

This rare variant of ice plains has large towers of ice and snow, which don't appear anywhere else in the game.

Extreme Hills

The extreme hills biome contains huge, steep mountains, but also has a lot of extra caves underground, making them good for resource hunting. Extreme hills are the only place where emerald ore can be found, and the only place where silverfish exist other than inside strongholds.

Swampland

Swamps have shallow, greenish water filled with lily pads, vines hanging off any trees, and lots of mushrooms. They're a good place to find clay, and the only place where witch huts are generated.

Taiga

A cold forest often covered in snow and composed entirely of spruce trees and small ferns, taiga biomes are the best place to find wolves. The mega taiga variant spawns incredibly tall trees, as well as mossy boulders and a rare dirt type called podzol.

Grass Plains

Grass plains are flat and full of long grass. They spawn large numbers of peaceful mobs, and are a common place to find NPC villages. They're also one of two biomes to spawn horses.

Sunflower Plains

These variants of grass plains are small patches of ground where huge numbers of sunflowers grow together.

Mushroom Island

One of the rarest biomes, mushroom islands are only found in the ocean and are made of mycelium instead of dirt. They're covered in all types of mushrooms, they're the only place where you can find mooshrooms, and no mobs spawn there – not even underground!

Jungle

Jungle biomes consist of tall, thick trees with dense leaf cover. Melons, cocoa pods and ocelots spawn only in jungles. Trees are normally covered in vines, which you can climb. You'll also find jungle temples in this biome.

Roofed Forest

Composed entirely of densely packed oak trees, roofed forests are the only place huge mushrooms spawn other than a mushroom island.

Desert

Deserts are made of sand above a base of sandstone. They have almost no animal or plant life apart from dead bushes and cacti, but contain lots of structures like villages, wells, and desert temples.

Savanna

These warm grasslands are the only place you can find acacia trees, and the second of two biomes where horses spawn naturally. It's a relatively flat and dry biome, and villages can generate here.

Savanna Plateau

A savanna variant with super-high mountains.

Mesa

Mesas are rocky, colourful deserts, and the only place you can find red sand, red sandstone and stained clay.

Deep Ocean

Twice as deep as normal oceans, and the only place you'll find ocean monuments.

Flower Forest

Variant of normal forest biomes, where the trees are replaced by flowers.

ESSENTIAL SURVIVAL TIPS

Taking those first steps in Minecraft can be daunting, especially if you're worried about taking them in the wrong direction. That's why we've put together this selection of tips that will help you make it past the first night and beyond. Ignore them at your peril!

Surviving in Minecraft isn't easy, especially early in the game when you might not be sure what you're doing. Here are a few things you can do to make sure your make it through those first few nights without too much trouble.

DON'T STRAY FAR FROM THE SPAWN POINT AT FIRST

Stay Near the Spawn Point
The place where you appear in a new world is called the spawn point. When you respawn after death, you'll return here automatically, so it makes sense to set up your base nearby, or at least create a cache of tools you can collect easily when the inevitable happens. Compasses always point here, so it's worth putting something useful near it.

You died!

urthworm fell from a high place
Score: 0

Respawn

Title screen

urthworm fell from a high place

DEATH IS ALL PART OF THE GAME!

Prepare to Die
Death in Minecraft isn't much fun, but it's going to happen to you. Even if you play in Peaceful mode, you can drown, fall into lava or drop off a too high ledge and end up visiting your maker with your pockets empty! It's all part of the game. The more you die, the more you'll learn how and when to stash your stuff away rather than risk losing it.

DIG STRAIGHT DOWN AND YOU COULD GET A FIERY SURPRISE!

Never Dig Straight Up or Down
Digging directly down might seem like the quickest way to get where you're going at first, but you only have to drop

into a hidden ravine or puncture a lava lake directly above you once to learn the hard way that it's not safe. Aim for the blocks just in front of you instead!

Burn Whatever You Can
When coal is in short supply, you'll want to make sure you cherish every lump you can find. Remember that you can burn almost anything wooden in a furnace, including old tools, saplings and sticks. Save the coal for making torches!

Turn On Your Night Lights
Wandering around in the dark might be fun at home, but that's because your house isn't full of monsters that screech and explode when they get too close to you (pet cats don't count!). In Minecraft, sunset is your reminder to get somewhere that has strong walls and good lighting.

Get Ready for Bed
As horrible as it sounds, as soon as you encounter some sheep in Minecraft you should kill them. The wool they drop will allow you to create a bed, which allows you to skip dangerous nights and annoying storms. It also sets a new spawn point, so if you die you return to the bed you last slept in (hopefully in your base!) instead of the place you started the game.

Protect Yourself
Iron armour is essential later on in the game, but early on it's hard to make. You can't make armour out of wood or stone, but you can make it out of leather. Chestplates are the most protective, but take eight resources to build. Iron and leather boots take just four resources and offer the same protection as a helmet, which takes five, so if you're trying to get armour fast, stick to boots!

Don't Get Lost
Early in the game, you may not have a compass, so if you go exploring, try to leave yourself pointers. Torches are good for this purpose because you can see them easily at night and from a distance, but any marker is helpful. Dig an arrow into the ground if you want to save resources!

RED SKY AT NIGHT, TIME TO AVOID A FIGHT!

BUILD A SHELTER AND PUT A BED IN THERE

A TRAIL OF TORCHES HELPS YOU NAVIGATE AT NIGHT

25

101 THINGS YOU NEED TO KNOW ABOUT MINECRAFT BLOCKS

Blocks are what Minecraft is all about, but as there are over 100 different ones, learning about each block and its uses can take forever! That's why we've put together this handy list.

LAVA FLOWS FURTHER IN THE NETHER

GRASS CAN BE TURNED INTO GRASS PATHS

PODZOL AND MYCELIUM ARE RARE DIRT VARIANTS

1 Lava will flow notably faster and further in the Nether than it will do in the Overworld.

2 Red sand is a variant of sand that you can only discover in Minecraft's mesa biomes.

3 Gravel has a one-in-10 chance of dropping flint instead of a gravel block when it is broken.

4 Purpur can be crafted out of chorus fruit, so in this case it literally does grow on trees!

5 You can plant podzol and mycelium on mushrooms even in direct sunlight.

6 Cobblestone is one of the most useful blocks in the whemple game. It features in no less than 17 different recipes!

7 Grass does not grow at all on coarse dirt.

8 Sheep can eat the grass off blocks to replenish their wool. Without grass, the blocks will then turn into dirt blocks.

9 Grass paths are flattened blocks, slightly smaller than a normal block, which you create by using a spade on grass blocks (rather than using the "break" button, which will dig it).

10 Coarse dirt can be made by mixing two gravel and two dirt blocks. It also generates in high mountains and mega taiga.

11 Farmland turns back into dirt if you jump on it too many times, if it's covered by another block, or if it dries out for too long.

12 Podzol and mycelium can't be crafted, but you can collect them from mega taiga and mushroom island biomes. You will need a Silk Touch shovel, though.

13 Mycelium spreads to other dirt blocks, like grass, but podzol doesn't.

14 Mycelium and podzol can't be tilled with a hoe to then make a farmland block.

15 Coarse dirt turns into normal dirt if tilled, and can then be turned into farmland.

BEDROCK CAN'T BE DESTROYED

MINING UNDERWATER MAKES YOU SLOW

YOU CAN'T DROWN IN LAVA!

16 Bedrock is the only naturally generated block in the whole game that can't be destroyed or collected.

17 In the Nether, bedrock forms a ceiling as well as a floor. It will burn forever if set on fire, just like Netherrack.

18 When your top half is submerged in water and you're standing on something, blocks take five times as long to break as when you're on land.

19 If you're not standing on something (i.e. sinking or swimming), blocks take 25 times as long to break!

20 Packed ice looks similar to regular ice blocks, but is opaque rather than transparent and appears in the ice spikes biome.

21 Even though it's a liquid, it's impossible to drown in lava. It's still not very safe, though!

22 Packed ice doesn't melt even if placed next to a light source.

23 If you collect coal ore (for example, with a Silk Touch pickaxe), you can then smelt it into coal.

24 Wood blocks can be used as fuel in furnaces, but it's more efficient to craft them into planks top use, than to burn them.

25 There's no difference between the various wood types, other than the colour of the planks they produce.

26 Leaf blocks will begin to disappear if they're not connected to a wood block within a four-block range.

27 Wood planks are the single most useful block in the entire game, as they feature in 28 different recipes.

28 Destroying a leaf block drops a sapling one in every 20 times. Jungle leaves only drop a sapling one in every 40 times, though.

29 Chiselled sandstone can be made by combining two sandstone slabs. Yellow chiselled sandstone depicts a creeper face. Red chiselled sandstone, meanwhile, depicts the wither.

30 If collected with a Silk Touch pickaxe, mushroom blocks can be used as fuel for smelting.

31 Redstone ore will give off low-level light (level 9) for around a minute if struck or walked over either by the player or a mob.

32 Snow layers can be stacked up to create partial blocks. Eight layers will create a full-size snow block.

33 Ice blocks cause you to slide, so if you sprint and hop you can then travel across them really quickly!

34 Ice and snow blocks will both melt if placed near a strong enough light source.

35 Ice and snow won't melt just from being in the sun, even when in a hot biome.

36 Even though cacti damage players and mobs that come into contact with them, you can mine cacti with your hand without actually taking any injuries.

37 The bottom of a cactus block doesn't damage the player – it's only the top and sides.

38 Once clay has been stained, it can't be reverted or recoloured ever again!

ALL THE SANDSTONE VARIANTS, INCLUDING CHISELLED SANDSTONE

YOU CAN BUILD UP SNOW LAYERS

MINE A CACTUS BY HAND

39 Grass will only spread to dirt if there's a light level of at least 4 on both of the blocks.

40 Red, orange, yellow, brown, white and light grey versions of hardened clay will generate in mesa biomes.

41 Mobs can also spawn on packed ice, which isn't possible on ice blocks.

42 Unlike the super-hard block in Minecraft, real-life obsidian is a glass-like mineral that's very easy to shatter.

43 Obsidian and bedrock are the only two blocks to appear in all three dimensions in the game.

44 Obsidian has a blast resistance of 6000, although blue wither skulls fired by the wither can destroy it on contact.

45 Sponges are only generated as part of ocean monuments, but they can also be dropped by elder guardians.

46 You can cook a wet sponge in a furnace to dry it out again.

47 If there's an empty bucket in the fuel slot when a furnace finishes drying out a sponge, it will turn it into a bucket of water.

48 TNT explosions can redirect things that are flying through the air, including falling sand and gravel, and arrows as well.

49 Bookshelves will power up enchantment tables if placed a single block away from them. To make the highest (level 30) enchantments, you need 15 bookshelves placed around the table.

50 Mycelium only spreads to dirt if the light level is at least 9 on both blocks.

51 Moss stone found in dungeons, mega taiga biomes and jungle temples can be used to craft mossy cobblestone walls.

52 Stairs aren't just useful for decoration or because they're compact – they also use reduce the player's hunger less than jumping the same distance up or down would.

53 On Christmas Eve, Christmas Day and Boxing Day, all chests will be given a "present" texture.

54 In a very old version of Minecraft from 2011, there was a "locked chest" block that couldn't be opened. One was generated in every chunk created between 1 and 5 April 2011, and displayed an April Fools' joke if you tried to open it.

55 You can place a trapped chest next to a normal chest, which is a good way to maximise your storage space.

56 Fences and walls are 1.5 blocks tall so that you can't hop over them.

57 Iron bars (and beds) lower the time it takes a zombie villager to heal.

58 Four iron bars in a square will create a gap big enough for the player to drop through them.

59 If you manage to break an End portal frame after activating the portal, it won't actually deactivate the portal.

60 Flower pots were added to the game based on a suggestion from a Minecraft player.

61 Cactus blocks that are placed in a flower pot will not injure the player.

62 Prismarine slowly cycles through 22 different colours in a process that takes five-and-a-half minutes to complete.

63 Nether quartz ore doesn't burn indefinitely, and has the same blast resistance as other types of ore.

64 You can craft glowstone without ever leaving the Overworld because witches will drop glowstone dust.

65 Grass blocks change colour depending on which biome they're in.

66 You can put carpet or snow on top of soul sand if you want to negate its effects.

67 If you walk on soul sand while you're in the Overworld, the sky gets visibly darker.

68 Netherrack is the softest form of stone. It can be mined by hand in two seconds.

69 End stone has quite a high blast resistance – 1.5 times that or normal stone.

70 End stone is impossible for endermen to move, making it a good defence against them.

71 Cakes are the only block that players can directly eat.

72 Enchantment tables are mostly made of obsidian, so they can't be destroyed by TNT.

73 You can find a single block of polished andesite in igloo basements.

OBSIDIAN IN THE END

THE MOSSY WALL VARIANT

SPONGE FILLS A BUCKET WITH WATER

Furnace

Inventory

74 You can climb up vines as if they're a ladder, but they won't slow you down when you walk through them like ladders do.

75 Ladders and wooden doors are the only wooden blocks that can't be used as furnace fuel.

76 You can turn stone bricks into cracked stone bricks by smelting them in a furnace.

77 Granite, diorite and andesite are identical to regular stone except for their visual appearance.

78 Vines have a small chance of spreading to a nearby block. They're most likely to spread downwards into air blocks, which will then form dangling vines.

79 Players can see through vines and sugar cane; mobs can't.

80 You can use bonemeal to force sugar cane to grow in the Pocket Edition, but not in the PC Edition.

81 Stained glass blocks can't be used in recipes that require glass blocks.

82 Hay bales are the only blocks that can be eaten by mobs. They heal up to 10 hearts when fed to a horse, donkey or mule.

83 If you fall onto a slime block, you'll bounce and take no damage from it.

84 Redstone lamps switch on instantly if powered by a redstone source, but take 0.2 seconds to turn off.

85 You can block the sound that comes out of a note block by covering the top of the block.

86 Nether portals deactivate if their frame is broken.

87 Passive mobs wander towards grass blocks, preferring them to anything other than a light source of 10 or above.

88 It takes 90 wood planks, 45 leather and 135 paper to build enough bookshelves for a level 30 enchantment.

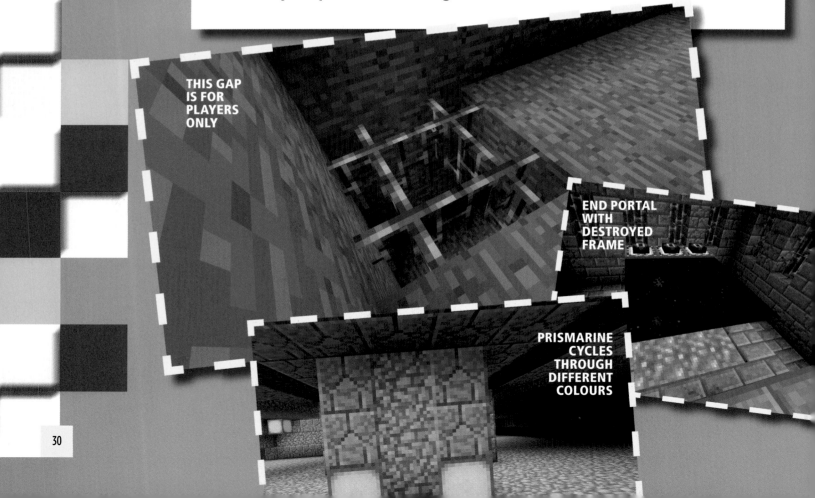

THIS GAP IS FOR PLAYERS ONLY

END PORTAL WITH DESTROYED FRAME

PRISMARINE CYCLES THROUGH DIFFERENT COLOURS

GRANITE, ANDESITE AND DIORITE REPLACE REGULAR STONE

JACK O'LANTERNS MAKE GOLEMS TOO

ONE OF 884,736 BEDS!

89 Jack O'Lanterns can be used to create snow and iron golems the same way that pumpkins can.

90 You can "dye" white wool using bonemeal as white dye, but nothing happens other than you losing the bonemeal!

91 The storage area of an ender chest is different for every player, so you can use them to hide items from other people in your multiplayer worlds.

92 Nether brick is immune to ghast fireballs, which makes it a good way to shelter while fighting one.

93 Cobblestone walls are slightly lower than fences, so when you connect a fence gate to a cobblestone wall it actually gets positioned lower.

94 End stone bricks are crafted out of four end stone blocks.

95 Carpets let light through, so you can place carpet on top of glowstone to make a room appear illuminated even if there's no obvious light source.

96 You can place carpet on top of farmland without destroying it, though this doesn't protect it from being jumped on.

97 Quartz blocks have a very low blast resistance (4), but two quartz slabs form a full block with a blast resistance of 30.

98 Mineral blocks like iron, gold, emerald, coal and diamond stack in piles of 64, so you can effectively carry 576 ingots/gems in one inventory slot.

99 Coal blocks fuel a furnace as long as 10 pieces of coal would, so you get a bonus piece for using them!

100 There are 884,736 different ways to craft a bed in Minecraft, but you'll always end up with the same item at the end of it!

101 If there's a hole within six blocks of a water source block, the flow is directed towards it.

FARMING, COOKING, FORAGING AND CRAFTING

Fancy A Bite To Eat?!

In Survival mode, if you want to get the most out of Minecraft, you're going to have to stay alive! To do that, you need to get on top of food for a start, and this chapter of our guide begins there. Furthermore, we're going to look at keeping clothes on your back, and the basics of crafting things – an essential skill in the world of Minecraft! Oh, and we might have a few pointers to help you get hold of a bit of treasure too!

WHERE TO FIND FOOD

Food is essential in Minecraft! If you don't eat, you'll starve. Simple. As you play the game, your hunger bar will empty, but once you eat it will be refilled.

If you play Minecraft in Survival mode (and don't play on Peaceful difficulty), you have to eat food to survive. Keeping your hunger bar full allows you to sprint and helps you regain health you've lost, so make sure you don't let it get too empty!

You can get food from farming crops or breeding and killing animals, but early in the game you may not have time for that. Here's the food you can get just by foraging!

YOU HAVE TO KEEP YOUR HUNGER BAR FULL

Apples

Apples restore four hunger points. Every time an oak leaf block breaks or decays (because you cut away any nearby wood), there's a 0.5% chance of it dropping an apple. If you're looking for food, this means you have to clear around 200 leaf blocks (about four trees) to find some. Leaves break quickly so it's not that hard!

APPLES ARE EASY TO COLLECT FROM TREES

Melons

In jungle biomes, you can find melons growing on the ground. They break into anything from 3-7 melon slices when mined and you can eat the slices straight away.

Each melon slice restores two hunger points when eaten. Remember to keep one, though, so that you can craft it into seeds and replant it!

Although similar to melons, the more common pumpkin can't be eaten directly, so isn't much good for foragers!

MELONS ONLY GROW IN JUNGLES, BUT THERE ARE USUALLY PLENTY THERE

BOTH MUSHROOM TYPES GROW IN SWAMPS

YOU CAN EAT BEETROOT AND CARROTS WITHOUT CRAFTING OR COOKING

Mushrooms

Mushrooms are easy to find in swamp and mushroom biomes. Some forests spawn huge mushrooms made of blocks that drop up to two mushrooms when they are broken.

You can combine red and brown mushrooms in a simple wooden bowl to create mushroom stew, which will restore six hunger points if eaten.

Village Crops

If you're lucky enough to find a village, you'll be able to take food from its farms, which have rows of wheat, carrots, beetroots and potatoes. Wheat can only be crafted into food, so it's not much use early on, but carrots, beetroots and potatoes all restore a few hunger points if eaten.

Eating a carrot restores three hunger points, eating a raw potato restores one hunger point, and eating a beetroot restores one hunger point. If you have a furnace handy, you can cook the potato to create a baked potato, which restores five hunger points.

Foraging Secrets

Sprinkle bone meal on small mushrooms to turn them into huge mushrooms as long as the conditions are right. If you surround an apple with eight gold ingots, you create a golden apple, which restores four hunger points and gives you the Absorption and Regeneration II status effects. Find golden apples in chests inside igloos, chest minecarts, dungeons and desert temples.

A GIANT MUSHROOM WILL GIVE YOU LOADS OF FOOD

HOW TO CRAFT FOOD

Keeping yourself fed in Minecraft is easier if you combine food items into larger meals. These recipes can take a little work, but usually fill up your hunger bar more than the ingredients would if you ate them separately.

Cake
To bake a cake, combine three wheat with three milk buckets, two sugar and one egg. Cake must be placed as a block before you eat it, and each block contains seven "slices". A slice restores two hunger points, so a cake restores 14 points.

Rabbit Stew
Craft together a baked potato, cooked rabbit, carrot and either type of mushroom to make a rabbit stew. You'll need a wooden bowl to keep it in, though! This stew restores more hunger in one go than any other food (10 points), and you'll be left with an empty bowl when you've eaten it.

Beetroot Soup
Six beetroots placed in a wooden bowl can be turned into beetroot soup, which is also known as "Borscht". Although it restores the same amount of hunger as the beetroots eaten separately (six points in total), the hunger bar will stay full longer if you combine them into a soup.

Pumpkin Pie
Combine a pumpkin with one sugar and one egg to make a pumpkin pie, which restores eight hunger points. This handy recipe combines three non-edible items into an edible one!

ANYONE CAN
TAKE A SLICE
OF CAKE!

Cookie
Combine two wheat with cocoa beans and you'll make eight cookies. They only restore two hunger points for every cookie though, and they don't make your hunger bar stay full for long.

However, they're useful as it's possible to craft them entirely out of things found in chests, so you may not have to go overground to actually make them.

Mushroom Soup
Mushrooms can't be eaten on their own, but you can combine two mushrooms in a wooden bowl to create mushroom stew, which restores six hunger points (the bowl can then be reused as well). Mushrooms are easy to find, so mushrooms stew is a good source of food.

If you're lucky enough to find a mooshroom, you can use a bowl to milk mushroom stew straight out of it!

Food Crafting Secrets
It's very easy to share cake with other players because it can be placed as a block – everyone can just walk up and take a piece!

Rabbit stew actually restores less hunger than the ingredients if eaten separately (13 points, excluding the non-edible mushroom), but it takes up less inventory space and is quicker to eat!

Pumpkins are the only item in the game that can be worn and eaten!

At the time of writing, beetroot soup isn't available in Console editions – only Pocket and PC editions.

PUMPKINS
- THE FOOD
YOU CAN
ALSO WEAR

FARMING

We all agree that hunting for animals is loads of fun, but you can't get away from the fact that it's time consuming. Also, natural herds are annoyingly slow to respawn. Once you start farming your animals, you'll wonder why you ever wasted precious time looking for food!

Farming Animals

If you want to survive long term in your Minecraft world, you need to start farming your own animals for food and resources. That means collecting and breeding herds of friendly mobs – not just for food, but for resources too!

Cows

Cows drop up to two leather and 1-3 beef. You can milk them (with a bucket) for milk, which can be used as an ingredient in cake or drunk to cure status effects. Cooked beef (steak) restores eight health points.

Mooshrooms are variants of cows found on mushroom islands. They drop steak and leather when killed, and can be milked with a bowl to make mushroom stew. Yum!

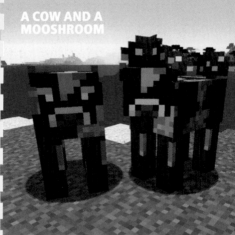
A COW AND A MOOSHROOM

A PIG AND SADDLED PIG

Pigs

Pigs drop one to three raw porkchops when killed. Place saddles on pigs to ride them, controlling their direction with a carrot on a stick, but they're slower than horses! If the pig has a saddle on its back, it will also drop a saddle when killed. Cooked porkchops restore eight health points.

Sheep

Sheep drop one wool if killed, but if you use shears to remove their wool they'll drop 1-3 wool, then regrow their coats later. In most versions, sheep will also drop 1-2 raw mutton when killed. Cooked mutton restores six health points.

A SHEEP AND A BALD SHEEP

ANIMALS

RABBITS HAVE SEVERAL DIFFERENT COATS

Rabbits

Rabbits drop up to one rabbit hide and up to one raw rabbit when killed. You can craft four rabbit hides into one leather, and raw rabbit can be cooked and eaten to restore five health.

Rabbits also have a small chance of dropping a rabbit's foot when killed. These can be filtered into an awkward potion to create a Potion of Leaping.

Chickens

Killing a chicken will get you up to two feathers and one raw chicken. A cooked chicken restores six health, and feathers can be crafted with flint and a stick to make arrows. You can also craft feathers with a book and ink sac to make a book & quill.

An adult chicken lays an egg every 5-10 minutes. Eggs can be thrown for the chance to hatch a new chicken, or used in recipes to make pumpkin pie or a cake.

KEEP CHICKENS AND YOU'LL GET EGGS, FEATHERS AND FOOD

Animal Farming Secrets

If you kill an animal by setting it on fire, it will drop the cooked version of its meat instead of the raw version, but the fire may destroy the item if you don't collect it quickly!

Cooked meat restores more hunger than raw meat, so don't eat food raw if you can help it!

Steak and porkchops are the most efficient way to regain health. Rabbit stew and cakes restore more health, but you can only carry one of each in an inventory slot.

Sheep regrow their wool by eating grass, so if there isn't any grass they'll remain bald!

SET A MOB ON FIRE TO COLLECT COOKED MEAT

Animal Breeding

To make two animals breed, you must attract a pair of adult animals then feed them the right food. They'll fall in love, shown by hearts appearing above their head. If two animals meet when they're in love, a baby version of the animal will spawn. Breeding animals also causes them to drop experience, which you can collect.

Once animals have bred, they can't breed again for five minutes. Baby animals take 20 minutes to grow to adults, but you may be able to speed this up by feeding them the food that makes their adult versions breed.

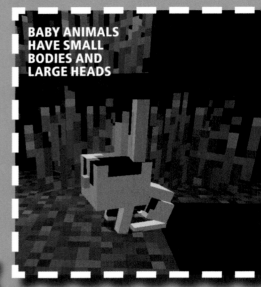

BABY ANIMALS HAVE SMALL BODIES AND LARGE HEADS

THIS SHEEP IS READY TO BREED

CHICKEN EGGS CAN HATCH WHEN THROWN

Animal Feeding

To breed horses and donkeys, you must feed them either a golden apple or a golden carrot. These can both be crafted by surrounding an apple with gold ingots or a carrot with gold nuggets.

To breed sheep, cows and mooshrooms, you must feed them wheat.

To breed pigs, you can feed them any of carrots, potatoes and beetroots (except in the Console Edition, where only carrots work).

To breed chickens, you can use seeds of any kind. You can also spawn baby chickens by collecting and throwing eggs – there's a one-in-eight chance that a thrown egg will hatch a chick, and a one-in-256 chance that it will hatch four chicks!

To breed rabbits, feed them carrots, golden carrots or dandelions.

Herding Animals

Whether you're breeding animals or killing them for their items (such as leather or pork chops), it's helpful to fence them into a tight space. To get them where you want, you can use a lead or entice them with the right type of food.

Leads are created out of four string and a slimeball, and can be attached to any non-hostile animal (except bats!). Leads stay attached to the animal until you remove them, and you can lead multiple animals at once using multiple leads. You can also attach leads to fenceposts to prevent animals from escaping.

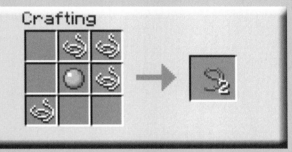

You entice animals to follow you using the item that makes them breed. Rabbits will also follow you if you hold dandelions!

RABBIT SKINS
CAN MATCH
THE BIOME

CHICKENS ARE
ATTRACTED
TO SEEDS

LEAD A SHEEP
TO WATER – OR
ANYWHERE ELSE
YOU LIKE

Breeding Secrets

It's possible to breed a horse with a donkey to create a mule, which is fast and strong like a horse and can carry a chest like a donkey. As in real life, mules can't breed with other horses.

When you breed sheep, their wool will (if possible) be coloured as a mixture of their parents' wool. This applies even if sheep have been dyed, so it's possible to create sheep of any colour in the game without using any extra dye by colouring then breeding the parents.

Most baby rabbits will have the same colour fur as one of their parents, but one-in-20 will have the fur pattern matching their biome instead.

Since meat is better at lowering hunger than vegetables, it's more efficient to breed and eat cows/chickens than it is to eat the wheat you'd feed to them.

Baby animals don't drop meat or other items when killed, and can't be bred. Baby sheep can't be sheared, but baby cows and mooshrooms can be milked.

TREES AND

Trees and flowers are useful in Minecraft, as they can give you essential resources, like wood blocks, which are needed early on to progress. There are many different kinds of trees and flowers, so here's our handy guide so you know how to grow them all!

FOUR SAPLINGS CAN GROW A LARGE TREE

Trees

Trees, made up of wood blocks and leaf blocks, are common in most biomes. When you break or mine wood from a tree, the leaves nearby will gradually begin to disappear. When leaf blocks disappear (or are destroyed), they have a chance of dropping a sapling, and the saplings can then be planted for the chance to grow another full-size tree.

MOST FORESTS CONTAIN JUST ONE TYPE OF TREE

Growing Trees

Getting a tree to grow is fairly easy: make sure there's enough light and space for the adult tree to fit in, and plant the sapling in a dirt block (podzol and grass also count). All trees attempt to grow at random intervals, usually several times a minute, but it takes around 30 minutes for a tree to grow from a sapling unless you help it along with bone meal.

You can transplant a sapling into any biome to grow the kind of tree you want. Giant tree variants can be grown by placing four saplings in a square and using bone meal on the cluster.

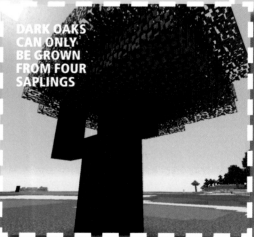

DARK OAKS CAN ONLY BE GROWN FROM FOUR SAPLINGS

Tree Secrets

There are six types of tree: oak, birch, acacia, spruce, jungle, and dark oak. The first three have no giant variants, but the other three do.

Dark oak saplings can't grow into trees on their own – you need four together to grow one tree.

Jungle trees only spawn as giant jungle trees, but you can grow a smaller version using a single sapling.

Jungle trees drop saplings half as often as most trees – a small jungle tree has a good chance of dropping none at all!

A REGULAR OAK NEXT TO SOME DARK OAKS

PLANTS

DANDELION

BLUE ORCHID

ALLIUM

AZURE BLUET

Wildflowers

There are 11 flower types. They can be crafted into dyes, or placed in the ground or a pot.

Dandelions: Yellow flowers found in any flower-growing biome (with the exception of swamps).

Poppies: Red flowers found in any flower-growing biome (with the exception of swamps).

Blue Orchids: Blue flowers that grow only in swamps.

Allium: Dark pink flowers that grow only in flower forests.

Azure Bluet, Tulips & Oxeye Daisies: Grow in plains, sunflower plains and flower forests. Tulips can be red, white, pink or orange.

Sunflowers: Yellow flowers that grow in sunflower plains and can't be grown by he player.

Lilac, Rose Bushes & Peonies: Grow in forests and flower forests.

LILAC

ROSE BUSH

WHITE TULIP

SUNFLOWER

Growing Flowers

All single-height flowers can be grown by the player – just use bone meal on bare grass blocks to create a scattering of tall grass and flowers common to that biome. While you can't grow double-height flowers, if you find one you can use bone meal on it to make one drop as an item, then replant it.

On Pocket Edition, using bone meal on a flower will cause more flowers of that type to grow around the existing one.

Flower Secrets

Iron golems will drop up to two poppies when killed.

Dandelions can be used to lead and attract rabbits.

The blooms on sunflowers move so they face the sun, even if you plant them underground!

PEONY

PINK TULIP

OXEYE DAISY

POPPY

ORANGE TULIP

RED TULIP

CROPS EXP

A variety of crops can be farmed by the player or found growing in villages in Minecraft. Some provide food, some you can trade or sell, and some you can use to make important utensils. We cover all the essentials and uncover a few secrets in our useful guide.

How To Grow Crops

Most crops need to be planted in farmland blocks. You can turn regular dirt or grass into farmland by tilling it with a hoe.

However, this is only the first step! You also need to make sure the farmland is wet. Farmland stays wet if there's a water source block within four blocks, as long as it's on the same level or one level above it.

Farmland also needs to be lit with a light level of 9 or higher. In the day, crops will grow normally, but at night you need to use torches or another light source to keep them growing. Crops won't grow when the player is asleep, or they walk too far away from where the crops are growing.

When your farmland is wet and well lit, you can plant your crops in it. Some crops (wheat, pumpkins, beetroots and melons) grow from seeds, but others (potatoes, cocoa beans, carrots and sugar cane) can be planted directly into blocks. Once planted, all crops grow from small plants into larger, more mature ones.

You can harvest the crop at any point, but if you wait until the plant is fully grown you'll get several items back instead of just what you planted. This gives you some to eat and some to replant – like real farming!

FARMLAND NEEDS TO BE NEAR WATER OR IT GOES DRY

PLANT YOUR CROPS AND WATCH THEM GROW!

SPEED UP GROWTH WITH BONEMEAL

LAINED

Melon & Pumpkin Plants

Melons and pumpkins are blocks rather than items, so they grow differently to other crops in the game. The seeds grow into a vine, and when the vine is fully mature it will generate one melon or pumpkin in one of the eight blocks next to it. When you collect the pumpkin or melon, the vine will generate another one the next time it grows.

Only the block with the vine in needs to be farmland, but take care to leave plenty of space around the vine. If it tries to generate a melon or pumpkin and can't because there's something in the way, the growth will fail and you'll have to wait for it to make another attempt.

Cocoa Pods

Cocoa beans are the only crop that doesn't grow in the ground. Instead, they can be planted onto jungle tree wood, where they'll grow into cocoa pods. A fully grown cocoa pod drops several cocoa beans when broken.

Sugar Cane

Sugar cane can be planted directly into grass, dirt, sand, podzol, coarse dirt or red sand as long as it's directly or diagonally next to a water block. The canes will grow until the plants are three blocks high.

To collect sugar cane, break the middle block. This will allow you to collect the available sugar cane but leave the base of the plant in place so that more will grow.

MELONS AND PUMPKINS GROW ON VINES, ONE AT A TIME

COCOA BEANS CAN BE "PLANTED" ON JUNGLE TREE WOOD IN ANY BIOME

SUGAR CANE IS COMMON NEAR WATER

45

Where To Find Crops

Wheat, beetroot, carrots and potatoes can all easily be found growing in small farms in villages, though not every farm contains every crop – it's random. Feel free to take a few, but try to leave some for the villagers. They'll harvest and replant the crops, meaning more for you later!

Wheat seeds (sometimes just called "seeds") can easily be collected by destroying long grass. Every piece of long grass you break has a one-in-10 chance of dropping seeds, so you shouldn't have to break a lot to find some.

You can craft pumpkin seeds out of pumpkin blocks, and melon seeds out of melon slices. Pumpkins grow wild in most grassy biomes, while melons only grow in jungle biomes (on the ground). Grab a few whenever you see them, and you'll soon have plenty.

Cocoa pods also only grow in jungle biomes, but on the trunks of jungle trees. It's possible to find cocoa beans in other places in the game, but if you encounter a jungle we suggest you don't leave without some!

If you can't find a farm or any crops growing wild, beetroot seeds, melon seeds, pumpkin seeds and cocoa beans can sometimes be found in chests. Zombies also have a rare chance to drop potatoes and carrots when they're killed.

Finally, sugar cane can be found next to water in most biomes, but nowhere else. It's easiest to spot in deserts where there aren't any trees to block your view.

VILLAGE FARMS ARE THE EASIEST SOURCE OF CROPS

COCOA PODS GROW IN JUNGLE BIOMES

PUMPKINS CAN GROW NATURALLY IN MOST BIOMES

Crop Secrets

One in every 50 potato plants you harvest in Minecraft will drop a poisonous potato, which is slightly greener than a normal potato and can't be planted or baked.

If you eat a poisonous potato, you have a 60% chance of getting the Poison effect for four seconds, which will in turn drain three of your health points.

Jumping or trampling on farmland can make it turn back into dirt, uprooting any crops that are planted in it. Remember to protect your farm from mobs!

Even friendly mobs can be a problem. Rabbits will eat mature carrot crops, for example!

You can craft bones into bonemeal and use it on immature plants to make them instantly advance several stages of growth.

Feeding wheat to horses restores one point of their health, but you can also craft nine wheat into a hay bale. If a horse eats a hay bale, it can restore up to 20 health!

You can quickly harvest lots of crops at once by flooding your farm with water. They'll be uprooted by the water flow, which saves a lot of clicking!

To speed up your crop growth, plant them in alternate rows instead of bunching single crops together. Crops grow slower if they're next to lots of crops of the same type.

You can mine pumpkin and melon blocks with anything (even your hand), but axes mine them the fastest.

Sugar cane plants have a small chance of being four blocks tall when they generate instead of three.

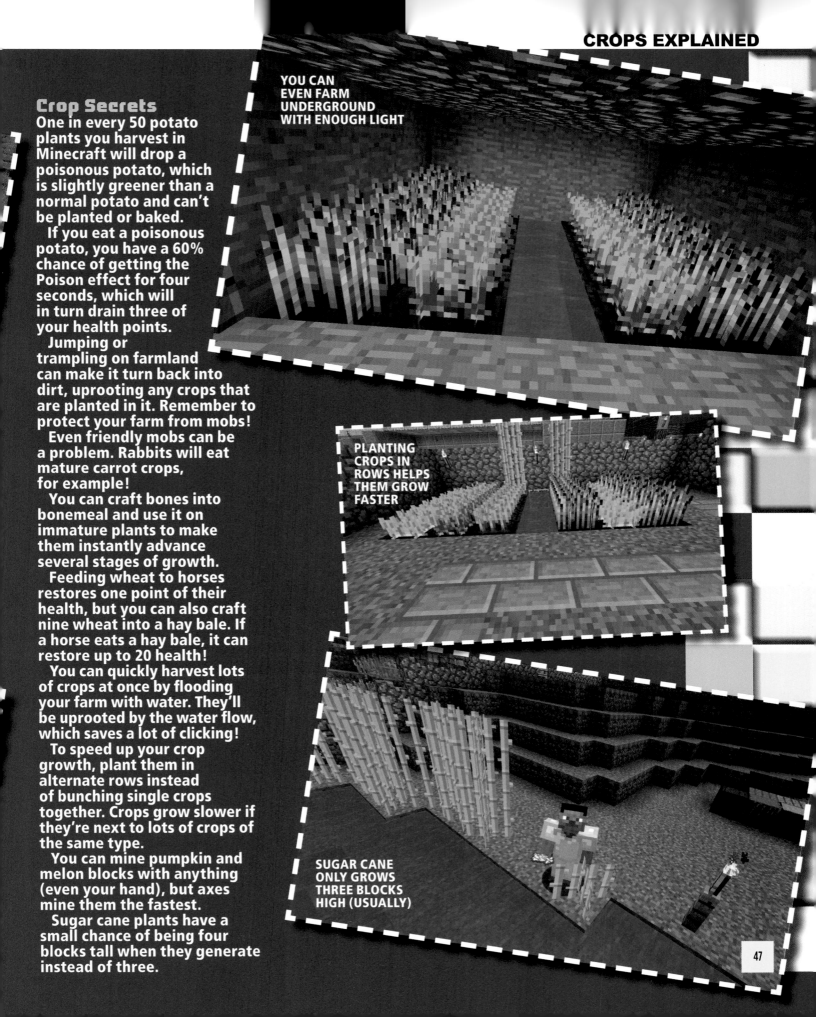

YOU CAN EVEN FARM UNDERGROUND WITH ENOUGH LIGHT

PLANTING CROPS IN ROWS HELPS THEM GROW FASTER

SUGAR CANE ONLY GROWS THREE BLOCKS HIGH (USUALLY)

47

HOW TO FISH

Fishing is a skill that's definitely worth learning in Minecraft, as it allows you to catch fish or other potentially useful items with just a fishing rod and a bit of patience!

How To Fish

You can easily make a fishing rod by combining string and sticks. You can fish in any still water, which makes it a great way to find items and food when you're underground.

To fish properly, cast your rod into the water and watch the red and white bobber. You'll see a trail head towards it then pull the bobber down under the surface. Reel it in as soon as this happens, and the fish will fly out of the water towards you.

You get 1-6 experience points for a successful catch, but if you reel in too early or late you won't get anything.

What You Can Catch

Fishing successfully gets you a fish, some junk or treasure. If you make 20 successful catches, on average you'll get fish 17 times, junk twice and treasure once.

On average, of the 17 fish you catch, 10-11 will be standard fish, 4-5 will be salmon and 2-3 will be pufferfish. Clownfish are the rarest – you'll have to catch 50 fish to get one!

Junk can be any of a bowl, unenchanted fishing rod, leather, leather boots, rotten flesh, stick, string, water bottle, bone, ink sac and tripwire hook.

Treasure will be one of an enchanted bow/book/fishing rod, name tag, saddle and lily pad.

YOU CAN FISH IN ANY WATER

IT'S A GREAT WAY TO GET FOOD EASILY

THERE'S TREASURE TO CATCH AS WELL!

Fishing Secrets

When fishing, it normally takes 5-45 seconds to catch something. The Lure enchantment can reduce this number by five seconds for every level (there are three levels in total).

The Luck of the Sea enchantment makes it slightly more likely that you'll catch treasure instead of junk or fish, but only by a tiny amount!

You can catch something with an unenchanted fishing rod 65 times before it ultimately breaks – it loses one durability point for each catch. Casting onto the ground will cause it to lose two durability points, and hooking a mob will cause it to lose three.

If you accidentally hit the ground or a mob, you can avoid losing durability by switching to another tool. The durability is only lost if you try to reel in!

If you give a fishing rod the Mending enchantment, it can be used forever. That's because catching anything with the rod will repair it at least as much as it's being damaged.

If you haven't yet earned the Cow Tipper achievement in the game, you can get it by reeling in a piece of leather.

It takes twice as long to get a bite when you fish in water that's not exposed in some way to sunlight or moonlight.

If it's raining, the wait time for getting a bite is reduced by about 20%, meaning you can make five catches in the time it normally takes you to get four (on average!).

The rarest item you can catch while fishing is another fishing rod. On average, only one-in-500 catches will result in you landing one! The most common item is the standard fish, which you'll get, on average, 51 times out of every 100 catches.

FISHING IN THE RAIN MEANS YOU GET BITES QUICKER

DON'T WORRY IF YOU MISS THE WATER!

YOU CAN FISH UNDERGROUND, BUT IT'S SLOWER

49

CLOTHING

Fancy changing how you look without having to use skins?
Simply craft some leather into armour, then dye it one of 12,326,391 different colours.
The possibilities are endless!

Making Clothing

You can make clothing by crafting leather into armour using the standard armour patterns, although once crafted they have a different name – cap rather than helmet, tunic rather than chestplate, pants rather than leggings.

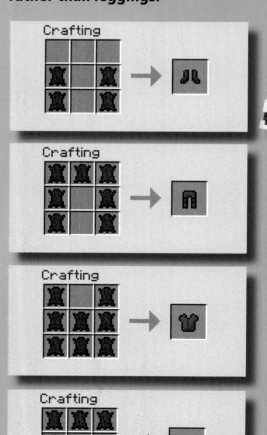

LEATHERWORKERS WILL SELL YOU CLOTHES

YOU CAN CATCH BOOTS WHILE FISHING

Clothes do count as armour, but they have very low durability and damage resistance. Leather clothing is half as resistant to damage as iron and less than half as durable, so is used mostly for decoration because it can be dyed into almost any colour!

Finding Clothing

Damaged leather boots can be caught as junk while fishing, and you can repair them either by combining them with other damaged boots or by patching them up with uncrafted leather using an anvil.

Leatherworker villagers will sell leather pants for 2-4 emeralds each. They'll also sell enchanted leather tunics as a second-tier trade as well for 7-12 emeralds.

Some mobs (zombies and skeletons, and their variants) will spawn wearing leather caps, tunics, pants and boots, and have a one-in-12 chance of dropping these when they die. They'll usually be badly damaged but may be enchanted. Leather is the second most common type of armour that mobs spawn with after gold.

GUIDE

Dyeing Clothes

Most flowers can be crafted into dye, which you can then use to change the colour of clothes. Some items, like red mushrooms and cacti, can be smelted into dye, and other items – lapis lazuli, ink sacs, bonemeal and cocoa beans – can be used as dye without any additional crafting required.

If you craft a piece of leather armour with some dye, the armour's colour will be affected by the dye. Unlike most dyed items, which can only take on one of the main 16 dye colours, you can dye coloured clothing again and again, and apply multiple dyes at the same time.

This means that you can dye leather armour into a total of 12,326,391 different colours, although many of them will look very similar to other ones! If you want to remove dye from leather armour, you can wash it in a cauldron full of water, which will revert it back to its original colour again.

Clothing & Dyeing Secrets

One thing you may not know about clothing is that it's quite easy to enchant compared to most armour, giving you a better chance of receiving useful or high-level enchantments. After gold armour, leather armour has the best chance of all of getting a good enchantment.

While some dye colours can be mixed, four can ONLY be made my mixing others: they are cyan (cactus green + lapis lazuli), purple (rose red + lapis lazuli), gray (ink sac + bonemeal) and lime (cactus green + bonemeal).

YOU CAN WASH OFF DYE IN CAULDRONS

SOME DYES CAN ONLY BE CRAFTED

YOU CAN CRAFT MULTIPLE DYES STRAIGHT ONTO LEATHER ARMOUR

TAMING

Fancy filling your home with dozens of cats to keep those irritating creepers at bay?
Or how cool would it be to have your own pack of loyal, tame wolves?
All you need to do is master the simple art of animal taming!

Taming Animals

Three of the game's mobs – horses, ocelots and wolves – can be tamed so that you can make use of them as allies. If you want to get them on your side, here's what you need to do!

HORSES ARE FAIRLY COMMON SO CHOOSE A GOOD ONE

Horses

Horses can be found in grassy, warm biomes and come in three forms: horses, mules and donkeys. All three can be tamed in the same way, and only when they're in their adult form.

First, approach the horse with an empty hand. Press the use button on the horse, and you'll get on its back. After a couple of seconds, the horse will probably buck you off. You may have to do it five or six times until the horse stops throwing you off. When the horse is tame, hearts will appear around its head to show that it's friendly.

You can tame horses more quickly by feeding them sugar, wheat, apples, golden carrots and golden apples.

All types of tame horse can be saddled and ridden, allowing you to cross long distances quickly. Full-size horses are great for combat because they can wear horse armour. Donkeys and mules can carry chests.

You have to breed mules – they don't occur naturally – but they're great all-rounders. They're faster and stronger than donkeys (not as strong as a horse) and they can carry a chest.

DONKEYS AND MULES CAN CARRY CHESTS

HORSES LOOK IMPRESSIVE WITH ARMOUR ON

ANIMALS

Ocelots

Ocelots are only found in jungle biomes. To tame an ocelot, first attract it by holding a raw fish and standing still as it approaches. The ocelot must be "begging" (looking at the player) and if you move too quickly it will get scared off. When it gets close enough, give it the fish. After you've fed it 1-3 times, it should become tame and change into a "cat", taking on one of three new coats. Cats are useful for scaring off creepers!

YOU CAN TAME OCELOTS INTO CATS

OCELOTS ARE NATURALLY FOUND IN THE JUNGLE BIOME

Wolves

Wolves appear in forest, taiga, mega taiga and cold taiga biomes, and are neutral if left alone. You can tame wolves by feeding them bones – usually it takes 1-3 bones to do this. If you hit a wolf, its entire pack will attack you, so be careful about which button you're pressing!

   When the wolf is tame, it will start wearing a collar and follow you around, sometimes helping you in fights. You can tame as many wolves as you like, and if you breed tame wolves they'll be born tame.

YOU CAN TAME WOLVES INTO DOGS

Animal Taming Secrets

Tamed wolves can be bred using any kind of meat (except fish), but will only breed if they're at full health. Tamed ocelots/cats can be bred using raw fish.

   You can use any type of dye to change the collar colouring of your tamed wolf.

   Ocelots are immune to fall damage, by the way!

TREASURE

The world of Minecraft is filled with riches to discover, some of which are kept in chests that can be found in lots of different locations. If you're looking for something specific, this guide will help you find exactly what you're looking for!

Chests are a great way to collect rare items without having to do a lot of work, so you'd better make sure you don't miss any! You can find chests full of loot in lots of different places. They all contain different items, so to help you know what to look for (and where!) here's a complete list of treasure chest locations.

Note that all lists of items are ordered from the most common loot to the most rare. Remember that most chests will contain a random selection of items from the lists given, not all of it. Anything marked in white is unique to the chest it's listed with.

BONUS CHESTS ARE SURROUNDED BY TORCHES TO MAKE THEM EASIER TO FIND

THERE ARE FOUR LUCRATIVE CHESTS INSIDE DESERT TEMPLES

Bonus Chests
If you generate a bonus chest with your world, it will appear near your spawn point surrounded by up to four torches. It can contain **sticks, wood planks, apples, acacia or dark oak wood, one of oak, spruce, birch or jungle wood, bread, raw salmon, wooden axes, wooden pickaxes, stone axes** and **stone pickaxes.**

Desert Temples
Desert temples contain four chests! Each can contain bones, rotten flesh, gunpowder, **sand**, string, gold ingots, **spider eyes**, iron ingots, emeralds, enchanted books, saddles, golden apples, iron horse armour, gold horse armour, diamonds, diamond horse armour and enchanted golden apples.

A DUNGEON USUALLY CONTAINS ONE OR TWO CHESTS

GUIDE

IGLOO BASEMENTS HAVE A CHEST IN THEM

Dungeons

Dungeons contain up to two chests with bones, rotten flesh, gunpowder, string, wheat, coal, redstone dust, beetroot/melon/pumpkin seeds, iron/gold ingots, bread, name tags, saddles, golden apples, music discs, buckets, iron horse armour, buckets, enchanted books, gold horse armour, diamond horse armour and enchanted golden apples.

Igloos

If an igloo has a hidden basement, you'll find a chest with coal, apples, wheat, gold nuggets, golden apples, rotten flesh, stone axes and emeralds.

BLACKSMITH WORKSHOPS HAVE CHESTS INSIDE

Jungle Temples

Jungle temples have two chests: one visible, one hidden. The loot in both contains bones, rotten flesh, gold/iron ingots, diamonds, emeralds, saddles, iron/gold/diamond horse armour and enchanted books.

CHEST MINECARTS WORK EXACTLY LIKE CHESTS

Villages

Village chests are found in the back room of any blacksmiths (rectangular buildings with flat stone tile roofs). They can contain apples, bread, iron ingots, oak saplings, obsidian, gold ingots, diamonds, iron boots, iron chestplate, iron helmet, iron leggings, iron pickaxe, iron sword, saddles, diamond horse armour, gold horse armour and iron horse armour.

Abandoned Mines

In abandoned mines, you'll occasionally find abandoned chest minecarts dotted around. Inside each one, there's the chance to find torches, rails, coal, lapis lazuli, redstone, bread, iron ingots, beetroot seeds, melon seeds, pumpkin seeds, activator rails, detector rails, powered rails, name tags, gold ingots, golden apples, diamonds, enchanted books, iron pickaxes and enchanted golden apples.

Strongholds

The size of strongholds means there are lots of items to find and three different types of chest that can appear, depending on the rooms the stronghold has. You can expect to find a good number of chests in any stronghold you visit!

Altar chests contain redstone, bread, iron ingots, apples, gold ingots, ender pearls, diamonds, iron pickaxes, iron boots, iron chestplate, iron helmet, iron leggings, iron swords, golden apples, saddles, diamond horse armour, gold horse armour, iron horse armour and enchanted books.

In libraries, the chests contain just a few items, but they're very rare: paper, books, enchanted books, compasses and empty maps.

Finally, storeroom chests can contain coal, redstone, bread, iron ingots, apples, gold ingot, enchanted books and iron pickaxes.

PLENTY OF CHESTS IN A NETHER FORTRESS – IF YOU SURVIVE!

STRONGHOLD LIBRARY CHESTS ARE FULL OF COOL GEAR

STRONGHOLD STOREROOM CHESTS ARE HARD TO FIND

Nether Fortresses

Chests in the Nether have lots of loot! You can find gold/iron ingots, Nether wart, diamonds, saddles, gold/iron/diamond horse armour, obsidian, flint and steel, golden chestplate, golden sword.

End Cities

They're only accessible late in the game, so chests here have the best loot by far. Expect to see gold/iron ingots, beetroot seeds, diamonds, emeralds, saddles, enchanted pickaxes, shovels, swords, helmets, chestplates, leggings and boots (all either iron or, less commonly, diamond), and all three types of different horse armour, shrinking in likelihood from gold to iron to diamond armour.

The Locked Chest

On April Fool's Day in 2011, the Minecraft developers added a "locked chest" to the game as a joke. For one week, anyone trying to open the chest would be told they had to buy a key from the Minecraft store and were redirected to a website. It was intended as a joke about paid-for downloads in modern games – there wasn't actually anything to buy at all, and the chest couldn't be opened!

THE FAKE LOCKED CHEST

Christmas Chests

In 2012, 2013 and 2014, if you played Minecraft between 24 and 26 December, all of the chests turned into giant presents. Small ones were red with a yellow bow, and big ones were green with a white bow. In 2014, the splash text also read "Merry X-Mas".

We don't know whether it will happen again this Christmas – it didn't in 2015 – but it's always worth looking out for it this Christmas!

CHESTS BECOME PRESENTS AT CHRISTMAS

REMEMBER TO GET THE ARROWS FROM THE DISPENSER

Treasure Secrets

In the Console Edition, bonus chests don't have acacia wood but can have pumpkin, melon and grass seeds, potatoes, carrots, cacti, both mushroom types and oak, birch, spruce and jungle saplings.

In Pocket Edition, dungeon chests can have ink sacs and cocoa beans. Jungle temples also contain dispensers (with a random number of arrows to steal!) Chests in Nether fortresses can appear by a bend in a corridor. Look around the corner before you rush to open them! In the Pocket Edition, village chests also include ink sacs and emeralds.

SWORDS & SORCERY:
THE COMPLETE COMBAT GUIDE

Ready For Battle?

Not every mob that you meet in a game of Minecraft will be a friendly one, so it's time we got you up to speed on combat. In the coming pages, we're going to look at tips and advice for attack and defence, as well as the importance of weapons and enchantments. Then, we're turning our attention to potions, which can be invaluable in the midst of a tricky battle! Special arrows come in useful too...

ATTACK &

Fighting enemies in Minecraft is vital if you want to gain experience, collect the items they drop and – let's face it – survive through the night! But as well as knowing how to attack, you have to know how to defend. Time to learn the essentials!

Weapons

There are two main weapons in the game: swords and a bow and arrow. Swords are good for up-close (melee) combat with players and monsters, while a bow and arrow can be used to attack from a distance.

There are also secondary weapons, like axes (which are used mainly for cutting wood but also deal a lot of melee damage), fire charges (which are one-time fireball projectiles), a flint and steel, and even snowballs! You can also use potions to fight, but we'll cover those in their own section later on!

Shields

Shields can be held either in your main hand or the "offhand" slot accessed through your inventory on the latest version of the game.

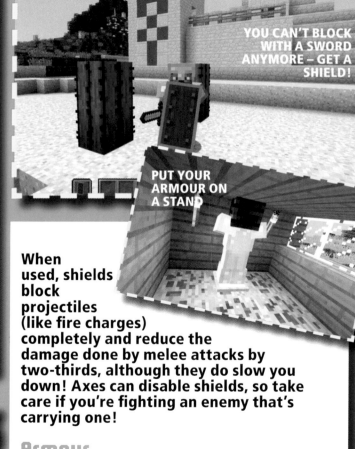

YOU CAN'T BLOCK WITH A SWORD ANYMORE – GET A SHIELD!

PUT YOUR ARMOUR ON A STAND

When used, shields block projectiles (like fire charges) completely and reduce the damage done by melee attacks by two-thirds, although they do slow you down! Axes can disable shields, so take care if you're fighting an enemy that's carrying one!

Armour

Wearing a suit of armour is essential for surviving any fight and should be your primary form of defence. Later in the game, you'll need to enchant your armour to make it strong enough to protect you during the most difficult fights, but for most of the game simple iron armour should be enough!

MOBS CAN USE WEAPONS TOO!

DEFENCE

Critical Hits

A critical hit is an attack that's 50% more powerful than a normal hit, so learning to use them is the best way to make sure fights end quickly! You can make a critical hit with any item, but the sword, axe and bow have the greatest gain from them.

To make a critical hit with a sword, axe or other handheld item, you have to jump and hit the mob or player as you fall back to the ground. You'll be able to spot that you've made a critical hit by the stars that will appear when your weapon connects with the enemy.

To make a critical hit with a bow, you have to release the arrow when it's fully "charged" (as in drawn back as far as it will go). In this case, you'll see the stars appear as a trail behind the arrow instead of when the arrow hits the enemy.

If you're using a diamond sword (the most powerful unenchanted weapon in the whole game), a critical hit can kill most enemies in two or three hits. The same is true of a bow and arrow: two direct critical hits will kill most enemies in the game!

There are some circumstances where critical hits won't happen. You can't make critical hits if you fall without jumping, if you're in water, if you're on a ladder, if you're riding a horse or pig, if you're sprinting or if you're affected by the Blindness status effect.

CRITICAL HITS MAKE STARS APPEAR WHEN THEY LAND

AN ARROW LEAVING A CRITICAL HIT TRAIL

YOU CAN'T LAND CRITICAL HITS IN WATER

Knockback

Some attacks cause a kind of knockback, which means that the enemy you hit will be thrown a block or two away from you. Usually, the stronger the attack (or the faster you're moving), the stronger the knockback is.

You can use knockback strategically. Knocking a mob into water might slow them down so that you can attack them more easily again, or you could deal further damage by causing them to fall off high ledges or into fire or lava.

Eggs and snowballs don't damage most mobs at all, but they do cause guaranteed knockback, which means you can use them as weapons.

Swords and axes deal the most knockback, throwing enemies around two-and-a-half blocks away from you if you hit them while sprinting. Other items (and your fists) deal around one-and-a-half blocks of knockback.

IRON GOLEMS ARE IMMUNE TO KNOCKBACK

MOBS ARE IMMUNE TO DAMAGE WHEN RED

SNOWBALLS DEAL PURE KNOCKBACK – NO DAMAGE!

Damage Immunity

When a mob is damaged, it will turn red for half a second. During this period, the mob can't take any more damage. Despite this, if you attack and hit the mob, your weapon won't lose durability, but it might prevent you making an attack when the mob is able to take damage, leaving you open to attack. It's therefore important not to just repeatedly attack too quickly!

Players also experience damage immunity, so you shouldn't get too badly overwhelmed if attacked by multiple mobs at once! Try to use the immunity to get away from whatever is attacking you, even if that means running towards a weaker enemy!

Attack & Defence Secrets

In the PC edition, axes do more damage than swords, but take longer to recover before you can use them again. They also lose two durability when they hit a mob or player instead of losing one durability like swords do.

In other editions, axes do less damage than a sword, but take less time to recover.

If you craft together a banner and a shield, the banner's pattern will then be applied to the shield itself, which is great for showing your allegiance during combat!

Note that armour and shields don't reduce damage from falls or drowning – only attacks from other mobs and players.

Critical hits affect all damageable entities – not just mobs and players, but paintings, boats and minecarts too.

If you're quick enough, you can avoid fall damage by exiting your world mid-fall. Then, when you reload, the fall will restart but its damage will only be calculated from the point you re-enter the game.

If you sprint while using an axe, the chance of it disabling a shield goes up substantially.

You can stop fall damage (without cheating!) by falling into water. If you drop onto slime blocks, you'll bounce back up, but eventually come to a stop without taking damage. If you fall onto hay bales, the damage will be reduced to 20% of its normal level.

A shield disabled by an axe attack takes five seconds to recover before it can be used again.

You can get the Sniper Duel achievement by killing a skeleton from more than 50 blocks away using an arrow, and the Archer achievement for killing a creeper with arrows (except on the PC edition).

AXES AND SWORDS ARE BOTH VERY POWERFUL

SURVIVE A LONG DROP BY AIMING FOR WATER

THE HEARTS SHOW HOW MUCH DAMAGE YOUR ATTACK DOES

UTILITY

Utility mobs – also called "golems" – are a special class of mob that can be crafted by the player. There are two types of golem in Minecraft: the snow golem and the iron golem.

What You Need

For snow golems, you need two blocks of snow and one pumpkin, and for iron golems, four blocks of iron and one pumpkin.

Blocks of snow are easy to find if you're near a snowy biome or a tall mountain. Use a spade to dig up a snow layer or two, then craft the snowballs you collect into blocks. You only need eight snowballs to make two blocks.

Blocks of iron can be crafted from iron ingots (nine per block), which means you'll have to collect or craft 36 ingots in total!

Getting pumpkins is harder. You can grow them from seeds or find them in the wild, but in both cases you can't do anything to speed up the process!

HOW TO MAKE A SNOW GOLEM

HOW TO MAKE AN IRON GOLEM

How To Make a Golem

To make a snow golem, place two blocks of snow on top of one another, then a pumpkin or Jack O'Lantern on top. It will instantly become a snowman-like snow golem.

To make an iron golem, place four iron blocks in a small "T" shape, then a pumpkin or Jack O'Lantern on top. It too will instantly become an iron golem. Note that the blocks either side of its "feet" and "head" also have to be empty. Even a snow layer on the ground can stop an iron golem from spawning properly, so remember to clear the ground before you activate them!

COLLECT SNOWBALLS FOR SNOW GOLEMS

MOBS

All About Golems

Golems are used mainly for protection – they attack hostile mobs and can act as an extra target for them. This gives you more time to attack (or escape!). Golems can also be put on leads and tied to posts to keep them in a specific area.

Snow golems have low health (they only have four points) and are weak. They throw snowballs at any hostile mob within 10 blocks, but the snowballs are only effective against blazes and the ender dragon. They ignore hostile wolves, but they do go after zombie pigmen.

Iron golems are stronger than snow golems. They have 100 health points and 4-31 attack strength. They can't drown and aren't hurt by falling, but will suffocate in solid blocks, and can be injured by lava and fire. Iron golems will attack mobs within 16 blocks, except for wolves and creepers.

Utility Mob Secrets

If a village has over 10 inhabitants, an iron golem can spawn automatically to protect it from attacking mobs (or players!).

When you craft a golem, the pumpkin or Jack O'Lantern has to be placed last. If you place the other blocks afterwards, it won't activate.

If snow golems enter a hot biome, stand in the rain or fall into water/lava, they melt.

In some editions, you can remove the pumpkin from a snow golem's head by using some shears.

SNOW GOLEMS LEAVE SNOW WHERE THEY WALK

IRON GOLEMS INTERACT WITH VILLAGERS

A SNOW GOLEM WITHOUT ITS MASK

SWORDS & AXES IN DEPTH

When you craft a weapon or tool, the material you use often determines how powerful it is. This matters most when you're making weapons. Here's how each material behaves and why you should use it.

Wood

Wooden swords are the weakest in the game, and most players never make one as it's very easy to get the stone to make a stone sword even if you're just starting out. Wooden swords deal four points of damage per hit, giving them a lifetime minimum damage of 240 points.

Wooden axes are more useful as weapons, at least early on, because they do more damage than swords. A wooden axe does seven points of damage per hit (as much as a diamond sword!) for a minimum lifetime damage value of 210 points. They have a 1.25 second cooldown time, making them joint slowest of the axes.

DON'T USE WOOD IN A FIGHT IF YOU CAN HELP IT

A WOODEN AXE IS WEAK, BUT STILL GOOD FOR TREES

Stone

Crafting a stone sword is possible almost immediately, so this might even be the first weapon you use in the game. A stone sword does five points of damage per hit for a lifetime minimum damage of 660 points.

Stone axes do nine points of damage per hit, which is more than even a diamond sword, and as much as both an iron and diamond axe. So even when iron is scarce, they still make an acceptable weapon. They can deal a minimum of 594 points over their lifetime and have a 1.25 second cooldown time, making them as slow as wooden axes.

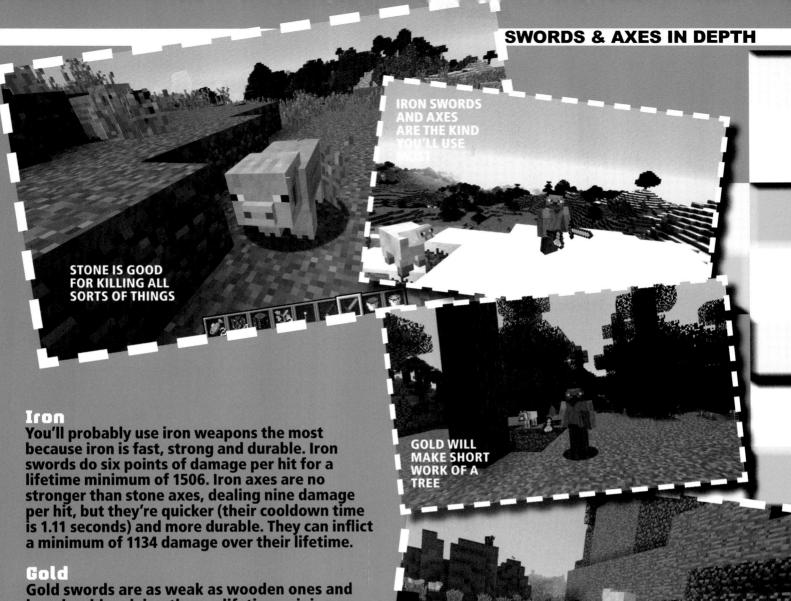

IRON SWORDS AND AXES ARE THE KIND YOU'LL USE MOST

STONE IS GOOD FOR KILLING ALL SORTS OF THINGS

GOLD WILL MAKE SHORT WORK OF A TREE

THIS DIAMOND SWORD WILL KILL A SHEEP FAST

Iron

You'll probably use iron weapons the most because iron is fast, strong and durable. Iron swords do six points of damage per hit for a lifetime minimum of 1506. Iron axes are no stronger than stone axes, dealing nine damage per hit, but they're quicker (their cooldown time is 1.11 seconds) and more durable. They can inflict a minimum of 1134 damage over their lifetime.

Gold

Gold swords are as weak as wooden ones and less durable, giving them a lifetime minimum damage of 132 points. Gold axes are also as weak as wooden axes, but they areslightly faster (they have a 1.0 second cooldown time). They do a minimum of 119 points of damage over their lifetime.

The main reason to use a gold sword or a gold axe (other than appearances!) is for easy enchantability. Like other gold tools and armour, you're more likely to get a good, high-level enchantment when compared to tools using another material.

Diamond

Diamond weapons are incredibly powerful. A diamond sword does the most damage (at seven points per hit) for a lifetime minimum of 10,934 points.

Diamond axes do nine points of damage per hit, which is no stronger than a stone or iron axe, but they have a 1.0 second cooldown time like gold axes, so they can do more damage in the same amount of time as stone or iron. They deal a minimum lifetime damage of 7029 points.

IMPORTANT NOTE

At the time of writing, the Console and Pocket editions use the old weapons system from PC versions before 1.9. Until they're updated, swords do one point more damage than stated and axes, instead of doing more damage than swords, do one point fewer than the sword in the same edition.

67

ARMOUR IN DEPTH

If you want to survive the hordes of monsters, you'd better make some armour – fast! Read on to find out the secrets of the various armour types you can choose.

To protect yourself against damage, you need to wear armour. Minecraft offers you the chance to use several different types of armour, but which of them is the best? And what makes one kind different from the others in the game?

Leather Armour

Leather can be collected in lots of ways: cows, horses and mooshrooms you kill in the Overworld will drop it, you can craft it out of rabbit skins, catch it while fishing, or buy it off leatherworker villagers. When you have enough leather, you can use it to create leather armour. Although it's the weakest grade of armour, it does have the ability to change colour if dyed, which no other armour does.

Some leather armour pieces have special names – helmets are called

CHAIN ARMOUR IS RARE AND DRAUGHTY!

caps, chestplates are called tunics, and leggings are called pants. This is because leather armour is really just another way of saying clothing! A full set of leather armour provides seven damage protection.

Chain Armour

Although it's quite weak, chain armour is considered special because it's quite hard to get hold of. You can't craft it from scratch, and have to either buy it from a blacksmith or kill a mob that's already wearing some to get it. A full set provides 12 damage protection.

While you can't create chain armour, it can be repaired using iron ingots and an anvil. Chain armour is the only kind of clothing that appears see-through when worn, and the helmets have a different design to the helmets of other armour types.

YOU CAN DYE LEATHER ARMOUR

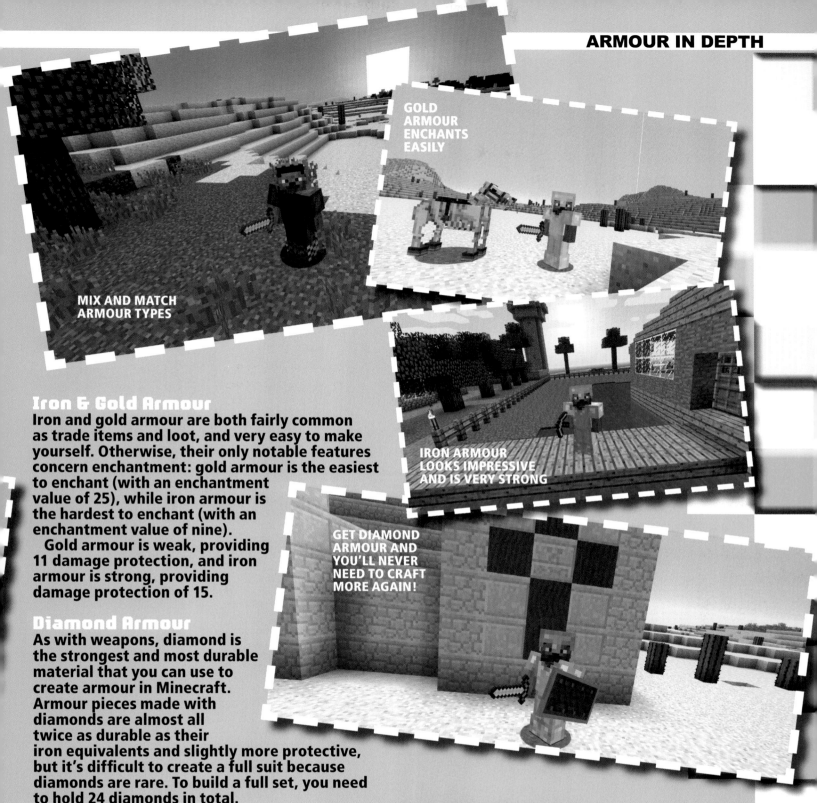

GOLD ARMOUR ENCHANTS EASILY

MIX AND MATCH ARMOUR TYPES

IRON ARMOUR LOOKS IMPRESSIVE AND IS VERY STRONG

GET DIAMOND ARMOUR AND YOU'LL NEVER NEED TO CRAFT MORE AGAIN!

Iron & Gold Armour

Iron and gold armour are both fairly common as trade items and loot, and very easy to make yourself. Otherwise, their only notable features concern enchantment: gold armour is the easiest to enchant (with an enchantment value of 25), while iron armour is the hardest to enchant (with an enchantment value of nine).

Gold armour is weak, providing 11 damage protection, and iron armour is strong, providing damage protection of 15.

Diamond Armour

As with weapons, diamond is the strongest and most durable material that you can use to create armour in Minecraft. Armour pieces made with diamonds are almost all twice as durable as their iron equivalents and slightly more protective, but it's difficult to create a full suit because diamonds are rare. To build a full set, you need to hold 24 diamonds in total.

Armour Secrets

The enchantability of armour, from least to most, goes iron (nine), diamond (10), chain (12), leather (15) and gold (25).

A full suit of diamond armour will protect players from 80% of attack damage. By comparison, iron only protects against 60% of damage, and leather just 28% of damage.

On Console and Pocket editions, you can get the Iron Man achievement by wearing a full suit of iron armour.

Zombies and skeletons can spawn with armour. Almost half the time it will be gold, with leather the next most common, then chain, then iron, and finally diamond.

Zombie pigmen and wither skeletons can collect and wear discarded armour, but don't spawn with it.

69

10 WAYS TO GET EXPERIENCE POINTS

Ever wondered how many experience points you'll get from killing certain mobs or mining different types of ore? We have the definitive guide to XP!

Experience points in Minecraft are used for several different things: you spend them when enchanting or repairing items, and the experience level you have can affect how good an enchantment is and how strong certain status effects are. For that reason, gaining experience is important for surviving and thriving.

You know you've collected experience when you see a flashing green and yellow orb appear, and hear a small chime as you collect it. Here are 10 ways you can get hold of them:

IF A TAME WOLF KILLS A MOB, YOU STILL GET EXPERIENCE

■ KILL SOME MOBS
Killing mobs is the easiest way to get experience. Most hostile mobs drop 5-10 experience points when you kill them, while tame mobs drop 1-3 experience points. Target mobs with equipment, as you get 1-3 points extra per item they're using.

■ LET YOUR WOLF OR OCELOT KILL A MOB
Mobs that fight or hunt on your behalf make the things they kill drop experience if they're successful in attacking them. Remember to collect the experience that gets dropped, as your tame mobs can't collect it for you.

■ SMASH A BOTTLE O' ENCHANTING
You can only get this rare potion by trading 3-11 emeralds with a cleric as a fourth-tier trade. When thrown against a solid block, it

THIS USED TO BE A CHICKEN, NOW IT'S A FEATHER AND EXPERIENCE POINTS!

SMASHING A SPAWNER GIVES YOU LOTS OF EXPERIENCE IN ONE GO

ORES DROP EXPERIENCE

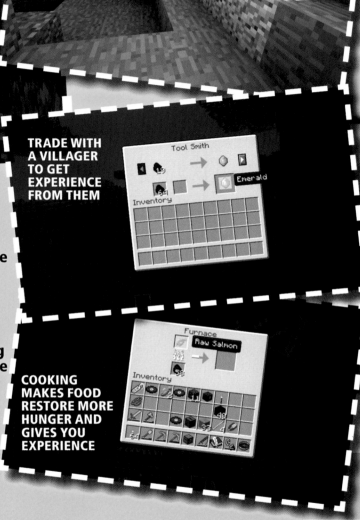

TRADE WITH A VILLAGER TO GET EXPERIENCE FROM THEM

COOKING MAKES FOOD RESTORE MORE HUNGER AND GIVES YOU EXPERIENCE

■ DESTROY A MONSTER SPAWNER

If you come across a monster spawner in a dungeon or abandoned mine, smashing it will give you 15-43 points, as long as you use a pickaxe to break it.

■ MINE SOME ORE

Experience isn't just about fighting. Mining ore will get you anywhere from 0-7 points, depending on the type. The types of ore that drop experience are coal (0-2 points), diamond and emerald (3-7 points), lapis lazuli and Nether quartz (2-5 points), and redstone (1-5 points).

■ SMELT SOME BLOCKS

Smelting blocks into resources gets you experience, although not always enough to generate an orb, so try to stack it up! If you smelt diamond, emerald or gold ore, you get one experience per block. Iron and redstone ore give 0.7 experience per block. Cobblestone, Netherrack, sand and stone bricks give you 0.1 experience per block.

■ BREED YOUR ANIMALS

Feeding friendly mobs like sheep, horses and chickens doesn't just get you baby animals, it also makes them drop anywhere from 1-7 experience points for every successful pairing. It takes a few minutes for animals to be ready to breed again, so it's not very efficient, but it's easy!

■ FISHING

Fishing isn't just a relaxing way to catch food – you also get experience for it. Every item you successfully reel in gets you 1-3 experience points.

■ TRADING

Successfully trading with villagers can get you 3-6 experience points per trade, and if the villagers are at maximum happiness (from lots of trading) you get even more: 8-11 points!

■ COOKING

Finally, if you want to get experience points just for staying alive, you can cook certain foods – potatoes, beef, chicken, fish, mutton, porkchops, rabbit and salmon – and get 0.35 experience for each item you successfully cook.

71

THE BEST ENCHANTMENTS

Learning to use enchantments is important if you want to survive the game's harder areas and fights, so here's a complete guide to what enchantments are available and how you get them!

ENCHANTING REQUIREMENTS

To enchant items, you need to have the following:

An enchantment table (4 x obsidian, 2 x diamond, 1 x book)
1-3 lapis lazuli ore per enchantment
Several experience Levels

Enchantment tables allow you to enchant your items. Place them onto the table along with some lapis lazuli, then you can "spend" your experience points and lapis lazuli to enchant them. Unfortunately, there's no way of knowing what an enchantment is before you apply it.

Optional: One or more books (3 x paper, 2 x leather)

Books can hold enchantments for safe keeping. Enchanting a book is a good way to make sure you don't apply a weak or uninteresting enchantment to a valuable tool or weapon.

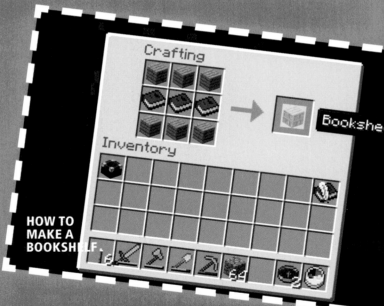

HOW TO MAKE A BOOKSHELF.

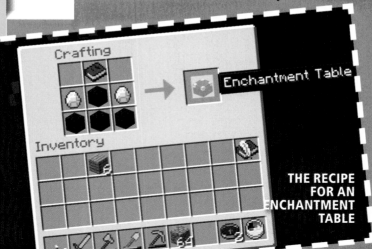

THE RECIPE FOR AN ENCHANTMENT TABLE

Optional: An anvil (3 x block of iron, 4 x iron ingot)

Anvils let you combine two enchanted items and keep their enchantments. You can also combine a book with an item to transfer the enchantment from the book to the item. This lets you add enchantments to items that can't be placed on an enchanting table (e.g. Unbreaking onto a fishing rod).

Optional: Bookshelves (6 x wood, 3 x book)

When placed around an enchanting table, bookshelves increase the level an enchantment can reach, but you have to spend more lapis lazuli and experience points to get higher level enchantments!

HOW TO ARRANGE YOUR ENCHANTMENT AREA

ENCHANTED ARMOUR GLOWS PURPLE

ARMOUR ENCHANTMENTS

The four main protection enchantments can be applied to armour. Each has four levels, and the higher the level, the stronger the protection offered.

No piece of armour can have more than one of the main four protection enchantments applied to it, but you can apply a different one to each piece of armour to give yourself all four protection effects at once.

Protection: Reduces all types of damage to the player, except damage caused by hunger.

Fire Protection: Reduces damage from fire sources, such as mob fireballs, flaming arrows, fires and lava.

Blast Protection: Reduces damage from explosions and also reduces explosion knockback as well.

Projectile Protection: Reduces damage from arrows, fireballs and other similar attacks too.

Other armour enchantments include:

Thorns: Covers you in spikes, giving you a chance to inflict 1-4 damage points on any mobs or players who attack you.

Depth Strider: For boots only. Increases your movement speed underwater.

Frost Walker: For boots only. Turns water near you into frosted ice. In upcoming versions, it will also protect you from damage from magma blocks.

Feather Falling: For boots only, this

YOU CAN'T TELL WHAT ENCHANTMENTS YOU'LL GET UNTIL YOU ACTIVATE THEM!

THE FROST WALKER ENCHANTMENT FREEZES WATER

enchantment reduces fall damage.

Respiration: For helmets only. You can hold your breath longer, don't suffocate as fast, and can see better underwater.

Aqua Affinity: For helmets only. You can break blocks as fast underwater as on land.

73

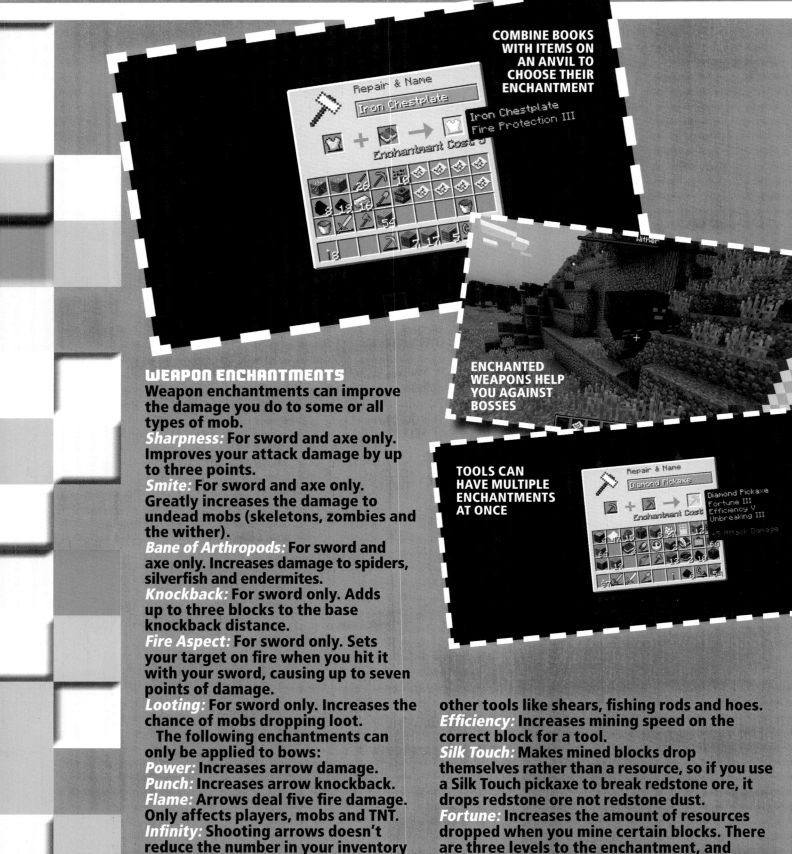

COMBINE BOOKS WITH ITEMS ON AN ANVIL TO CHOOSE THEIR ENCHANTMENT

Repair & Name

Iron Chestplate

Iron Chestplate
Fire Protection III

Enchantment Cost

ENCHANTED WEAPONS HELP YOU AGAINST BOSSES

TOOLS CAN HAVE MULTIPLE ENCHANTMENTS AT ONCE

Repair & Name

Diamond Pickaxe

Diamond Pickaxe
Fortune III
Efficiency V
Unbreaking III

Enchantment Cost

+5 Attack Damage

WEAPON ENCHANTMENTS

Weapon enchantments can improve the damage you do to some or all types of mob.

Sharpness: For sword and axe only. Improves your attack damage by up to three points.

Smite: For sword and axe only. Greatly increases the damage to undead mobs (skeletons, zombies and the wither).

Bane of Arthropods: For sword and axe only. Increases damage to spiders, silverfish and endermites.

Knockback: For sword only. Adds up to three blocks to the base knockback distance.

Fire Aspect: For sword only. Sets your target on fire when you hit it with your sword, causing up to seven points of damage.

Looting: For sword only. Increases the chance of mobs dropping loot.

The following enchantments can only be applied to bows:

Power: Increases arrow damage.

Punch: Increases arrow knockback.

Flame: Arrows deal five fire damage. Only affects players, mobs and TNT.

Infinity: Shooting arrows doesn't reduce the number in your inventory (regular arrows only!).

TOOL ENCHANTMENTS

Tool enchantments can be applied to pickaxes, axes and shovels (unless otherwise noted) and sometimes other tools like shears, fishing rods and hoes.

Efficiency: Increases mining speed on the correct block for a tool.

Silk Touch: Makes mined blocks drop themselves rather than a resource, so if you use a Silk Touch pickaxe to break redstone ore, it drops redstone ore not redstone dust.

Fortune: Increases the amount of resources dropped when you mine certain blocks. There are three levels to the enchantment, and higher levels cause more drops.

Luck of the Sea: For fishing rod only. Lowers the chance of catching junk and fish, and increases the chance of catching treasure.

Lure: For fishing rod only. Speeds up fish bites by five seconds a level.

A FULLY POWERED-UP ENCHANTMENT TABLE APPLIES HIGH-LEVEL ENCHANTMENTS

ANVILS ALLOW YOU TO REPAIR ITEMS WITHOUT LOSING THEIR ENCHANTMENTS

ALREADY ENCHANTED TOOLS CAN BE FOUND IN SOME CHESTS

Chest
Diamond Pickaxe
Mending
Unbreaking III

When in main hand:
1.2 Attack Speed
5 Attack Damage

UNBREAKING & MENDING

Although most enchantments are restricted to either tools, weapons or amour, two can be applied to any breakable equipment, including carrot on a stick, flint and steel, shields and elytra, which accept no others: Unbreaking and Mending

Unbreaking is a special enchantment that improves the durability of any item it's cast on. If an item would normally lose multiple points of durability for its use, such as hooking a mob with a fishing rod, the Unbreaking enchantment applies individually to each point of durability lost.

Mending works in a different way: it uses every experience point you collect to repair two durability on a worn item. If the item isn't worn, the experience points will be added to your total as normal, and if multiple items in your inventory have the enchantment the points will be applied to one randomly.

ENCHANTMENT TIPS & SECRETS

Only diamond items can hold a level V enchantment. This restriction affects five enchantments in total. They are: Efficiency, Power, Bane of Arthropods, Smite and Sharpness.

Enchanted items glow purple. Select them in your inventory to see which enchantment (or enchantments) they currently hold.

Items made out of gold are more likely to get high-level enchantments than those made of iron, diamond, wood and leather. Unfortunately, gold tools and armour break very easily, so the benefits of doing this are quite small.

Remember that if you repair an enchanted item on a crafting grid, you'll lose its enchantment, even if they both hold the same one. To retain enchantments, repair items on an anvil instead.

BREWING GUIDE

Potions can be made out of a variety of materials in Minecraft to give you special abilities. All you need is a brewing stand, a few glass bottles and some Nether wart to get started!

To start brewing, just craft yourself a brewing stand (blaze rod + three cobblestone) or collect one from an igloo basement. You also need several glass bottles (3 x glass blocks) and water to fill them. Also collect Nether wart and blaze rods from a Nether fortress.

STEP ONE: BASE POTIONS
To make your base potions, fill your glass bottles with water then place them into a brewing stand. Add blaze powder (on the PC edition) to power the brewing process. Next, brew a potion by adding a fermented spider eye (sugar + mushroom + spider eye) to make a Potion of Weakness (which reduces damage dealt by 50%), or Nether wart to make an awkward potion. Gunpowder creates a splash water potion, which can put out fires when thrown.

KEEP EVERYTHING YOU NEED CLOSE BY

ALL THE BREWING EQUIPMENT YOU NEED

STEP TWO: MORE INGREDIENTS
If you have an awkward potion, you can add the following to then create a working potion:

Golden carrot = Potion of Night Vision (lets you see in the dark)
Magma cream = Potion of Fire Resistance (reduces fire damage)
Rabbit's foot = Potion of Leaping (increases jump height)
Sugar = Potion of Swiftness (increases player speed)
Pufferfish = Potion of Water Breathing (increases breath underwater)
Glistering melon = Potion of Healing (instantly recovers health)
Spider eye = Potion of Poison (deals damage)
Ghast tear = Potion of Regeneration (recovers health over time)
Blaze powder = Potion of Strength (increases damage dealt by 130%)

WITCHES ARE THE ONLY MOB WITH THEIR OWN POTIONS

BREW DRINKABLE POTIONS BY FILTERING ITEMS INTO WATER BOTTLES

STEP THREE: EXTENDING & ALTERING POTIONS

You can now take the potions out of the brewing stand and use them, but their effects will be weak. Most potions brewed at this stage have effects that last for three minutes, but some for as little as 45 seconds.

To create stronger/extended potions, you can add extra ingredients. Adding redstone can usually double the time a potion's effects last for, while adding glowstone dust makes the effects stronger, but halves the time they last for.

You can also add fermented spider eyes to "corrupt" a potion's effects:

Potion of Night Vision becomes Potion of Invisibility (that makes its target disappear)

Potion of Swiftness & Leaping becomes Potion of Slowness (which slows down its target)

Potion of Healing & Poison becomes Potion of Harming (which then deals instant damage).

You can also add gunpowder to make a splash potion, and dragon's breath to make a lingering potion, but we'll discuss those more later!

POTION & BREWING SECRETS

One piece of blaze powder can power around 20 brewing operations, so you don't need huge amounts of it!

You don't have to craft glass bottles – you can collect them by killing witches,

YOU NEED NETHER WART TO BREW POTIONS

THERE ARE LOTS OF POTIONS – SOME CAN'T BE CRAFTED YET!

who drop 0-6 empty bottles when they die.

Adding brewing ingredients to a water bottle rather than an awkward potion creates either a mundane or thick potion, both of which are useless.

You can use a cauldron to fill water bottles in the Nether, where there's no other source of water.

SPLASH POTIONS

Not all drinkable potions are much use. You don't usually want to drink a Potion of Weakness, for example! Instead, you can turn it into a throwable potion called a "splash potion".

GETTING & USING GUNPOWDER

To create a splash potion, you need to collect gunpowder. Gunpowder is dropped by creepers, ghasts and witches when you kill them, and can also be found inside desert temple chests and jungle temple chests. When you have the gunpowder, all you need to do is filter it into an existing potion on a brewing stand to turn it into a splash potion.

THROWING SPLASH POTIONS

Once your potion has been turned into a splash potion, its bottle will take on a curved shape. Splash potions are thrown (the same way eggs and snowballs can be thrown), but instead of placing their effect on you, their effects will be applied to any player or mob

THROW A SPLASH POTION AT YOUR ENEMIES

within a small distance of where the bottle lands.

You can use this effect to great advantage. It allows you to weaken or slow down your enemies, or you can heal and protect allies. Perhaps most usefully, the potion can affect multiple mobs and players at once as long as they're standing close enough to the place where the potion smashes.

It's particularly recommended that you turn potions which deal negative effects into splash potions – it's unlikely you'd ever want to make yourself slower, weaker or poisoned, for instance!

GET GUNPOWDER BY KILLING CREEPERS

IT CAN AFFECT
MULTIPLE MOBS
AT ONCE

SPLASH WATER
BOTTLES PUT
OUT FIRES

THE EFFECT
DECREASES
THE FURTHER
AWAY A MOB IS
STANDING

YOU CAN
COLLECT A FREE
SPLASH POTION
IN HALF OF ALL
IGLOOS

SPLASH POTION SECRETS

Make sure you take care when throwing splash potions because if they land too close to you, you can be affected by them. You can even accidentally heal nearby enemies if you use one to try and heal yourself!

It's possible to create a splash mundane potion or a splash thick potion, but these will have no effect when thrown.

All splash potions have slightly different effects to their drinkable versions. In particular, they last for three-quarters the amount of time, so if a potion's effect lasts for one minute when you drink it, the splash potion version will only last for 45 seconds.

The blast range of a splash potion can also affect its power. The effect will extend four blocks in every direction from the place the potion smashed, and a direct hit on a player or mob will give it 100% of the potion's effect. This amount decreases the further away a player or mob is from the potion when it breaks.

Splash water potions can be used to put out fires on the block they hit and the four immediately adjacent to it, but won't affect mobs that are harmed by water such as blazes and endermen.

One of the few potions you can find in Minecraft without crafting is a Splash Potion of Weakness, which appears in the basement of igloos.

Remember that potion effects aren't always obvious. Undead mobs like zombies and skeletons are injured by Splash Potions of Healing, and healed by Splash Potions of Harming!

LINGERING POTIONS

If splash potions are too easy to miss for your liking, why not brew a lingering potion instead? These are difficult to brew because of what you have to collect, but the danger is worth it!

WHAT YOU NEED

The key ingredient of a lingering potion is dragon's breath, which can only be obtained from one place: the ender dragon. When it shoots an acid ball, the resulting attack remains in a pool on the ground for a few seconds.

At this point, you have to use an empty glass bottle on the purple particles to collect the dragon's breath. If successful, your bottle will be full and you can repeat the process as many times as you like. We recommend you give it a few goes just to make the trip worth it!

Once you have enough dragon's breath, you must defeat the dragon and return to the Overworld so that you can start brewing.

LINGERING POTIONS CAN AFFECT MULTIPLE MOBS

YOU NEED TO COLLECT DRAGON'S BREATH TO MAKE LINGERING POTIONS

BREWING LINGERING POTIONS

To brew a lingering potion, you need to place a splash potion in the bottom of your brewing stand and the dragon's breath bottle in the top. The splash potion will then be converted into a lingering potion, which has a different, smaller-shaped bottle.

As with all brewing, you also need blaze powder to power the operation. If brewing a lingering potion, you should try to make sure all three slots in the brewing stand are full, otherwise you're wasting good dragon's breath!

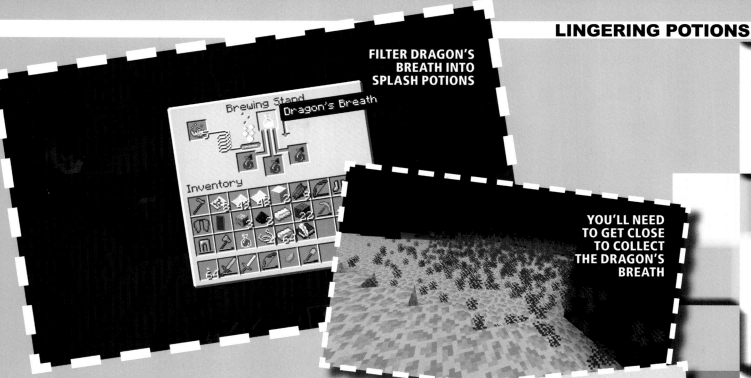

FILTER DRAGON'S BREATH INTO SPLASH POTIONS

YOU'LL NEED TO GET CLOSE TO COLLECT THE DRAGON'S BREATH

USAGE

When thrown, lingering potions remain in a pool on the ground, like dragon's breath does, allowing them to affect multiple mobs and players over a longer period of time than splash potions.

The pool made by a splash potion covers three blocks at first, then slowly shrinks over the next 30 seconds. Any mob or player that touches the pool will get the appropriate status effect, but will also instantly shrink the pool by half a block.

If a potion has a limited duration, the effects of a lingering potion will last for half as long as a normal potion. If the potion has instant effects, a lingering potion is half as powerful as the corresponding drinkable potion.

A lingering potion is good to use in enclosed spaces, where mobs have no choice but to walk through it in order to get to you, or if you have multiple players to heal/power up who are all in the same place.

LINGERING POTION SECRETS

At the time of writing, lingering potions are only available on the PC edition, although they'll be added to other versions of the game in future.

Lingering potions are essential in crafting tipped arrows, as you can find out on the next page!

REMEMBER TO TAKE A GLASS BOTTLE!

LINGERING POTIONS ARE DIFFERENT COLOURS DEPENDING ON THEIR POTION TYPE

The pool colour of a lingering potion will match the colour of the potion itself.

As with splash potions, you can create lingering potions from water bottles, mundane potions, thick potions and awkward potions, but they will have no effect unless combined with an actual ingredient.

81

SPECIAL ARROWS

The latest edition of Minecraft supports two new types of arrow: tipped and spectral. These are currently unavailable in the Pocket or Console editions, but keep reading as we're sure they'll be available eventually and it's worth knowing about them!

CRAFTING TIPPED ARROWS

Tipped arrows are crafted by surrounding a lingering potion with up to eight normal arrows. The potion is consumed and the arrows then become a stack of up to eight tipped arrows.

This recipe makes them hard to produce in great numbers (because dragon's breath, the main ingredient of a lingering potion, isn't easy to come by), but if you do you'll have access to some powerful weapons!

The craftable types of tipped arrow are as follows:

- Arrow of Regeneration
- Arrow of Swiftness
- Arrow of Fire Resistance
- Arrow of Healing
- Arrow of Night Vision
- Arrow of Strength

YOU NEED LINGERING POTIONS TO CRAFT TIPPED ARROWS

- Arrow of Leaping
- Arrow of Invisibility
- Arrow of Poison
- Arrow of Weakness
- Arrow of Slowness
- Arrow of Harming
- Arrow of Water Breathing

The effect of a tipped arrow only lasts one-eighth as long as a corresponding potion and isn't affected by the strength of the arrow itself. The arrows still cause normal damage when they strike their target, but cause a lot more damage than a normal arrow and have a longer range than splash or lingering potions.

Unlike regular arrows, the Infinity enchantment won't affect tipped arrows.

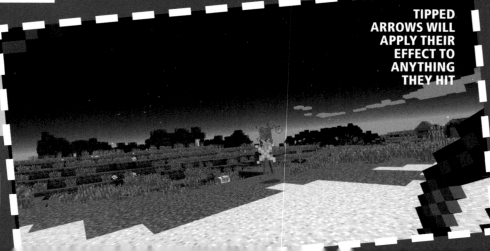

TIPPED ARROWS WILL APPLY THEIR EFFECT TO ANYTHING THEY HIT

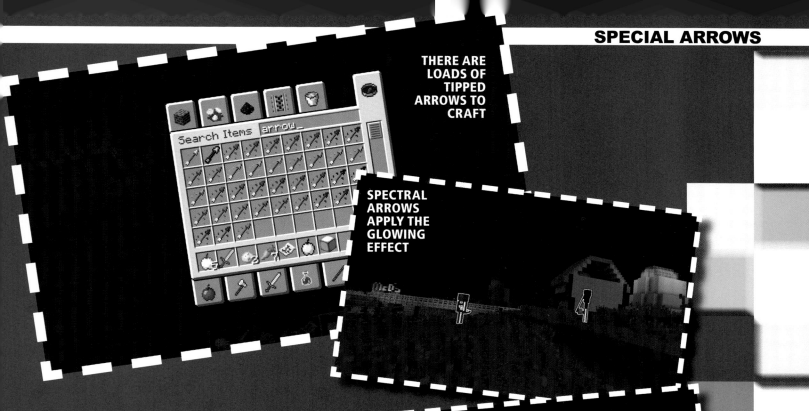

THERE ARE LOADS OF TIPPED ARROWS TO CRAFT

SPECTRAL ARROWS APPLY THE GLOWING EFFECT

THE GLOWING EFFECT CAN BE SEEN THROUGH BLOCKS

SPECTRAL ARROWS

If you place four pieces of glowstone dust around a regular arrow, you'll create two spectral arrows. Spectral arrows imbue any mob or player that they hit with the Glowing status effect for 10 seconds. The effect creates an outline around the mob, which is visible even through blocks, meaning it's possible to track them when you can't see them.

If the target has been assigned a team in multiplayer, the outline will be the corresponding colour, otherwise it will be white. The arrow is designed to let you track escaping players and mobs who might try to hide, and doesn't do extra damage.

Like tipped arrows, spectral arrows will still be consumed if the Infinity enchantment is active on your bow.

SPECIAL ARROW SECRETS

There are two types of tipped arrow in the game that currently cannot be crafted:

The Arrow of Luck uses the luck potion, which isn't yet craftable, and it alters the player's chance of finding good loot in a treasure chest, although it probably wouldn't be that much use in an arrow!

The Arrow of Splashing would theoretically be created by crafting a lingering water bottle with an arrow,

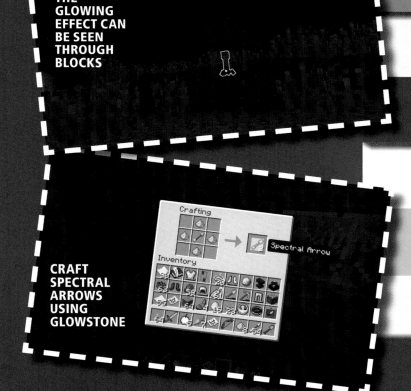

CRAFT SPECTRAL ARROWS USING GLOWSTONE

but this currently can't be done. It has no effect to apply and may not ever be added to the game properly, but can be obtained using the console!

A Potion of Glowing also exists in Minecraft's code, but, again, can't be obtained without using the console. This might change in future, but it's hard to say!

UNCHARTED MINECRAFT:

EXPLORATION HINTS

Time For An Adventure!

Not everything in Minecraft is to do with battling mobs or making sure you've got enough food to stay alive! There's also the fun of exploring the game world, and in this chapter we're going to take you through some of the many delights you may meet on your Minecraft travels! From the secrets of the likes of strongholds and temples to what you need to know about villages and the Nether, we've got a lot to get through!

NAVIGATION &

The Overworld stretches on forever, as far as the eye can see, so making sure you know where you are is important. To avoid getting lost, you need to learn how to navigate – and there are a few tricks and tools that can help!

COMPASS

A compass can be made quite easily in the game – simply surround a piece of redstone with iron ingots. When you've crafted it, the red hand of the compass will always point towards your world's original spawn point. As such, while you might not be able to find your way to a specific place, you can always find your way to somewhere familiar.

The compass works whether you're holding it or looking at it in your inventory, so many like to keep one in their quick-select bar where it can be glanced at. There's no distance limit on the compass, so as long as you keep the red hand pointing in front of you, you'll get to a place you've been to before.

CLOCKS

You can craft a clock using redstone and gold ingots, and when it's made you can use it to help you manage your time when you're exploring. If you're underground, experiencing a storm or in a dimly lit forest, having a reminder that night is coming might be the signal you need to get somewhere safe!

You can place clocks in an item frame to make a wall clock, which will always show the correct time.

HOLD A COMPASS IN EITHER HAND - OR BOTH!

EXPLORATION

MAPS

Maps are great for seeing what's around you and orienting yourself in your world. To craft a blank map, you must surround a compass with blank paper. To fill in a blank map, you just have to look at it and the area around you will appear automatically. Wander about until the map is full, and you've got a useful picture of what's around you.

However, the first map you make has a scale of one map pixel to one block, which is normally too small to be useful. You can craft a map with a smaller scale by surrounding it with eight pieces of paper. You can do this several more times to create a map where one map pixel represents 16 blocks.

Maps are oriented with north at the top. You appear on the map as a white pointer, and a green pointer shows the location of any framed maps.

NAVIGATION SECRETS

Clocks and compasses don't work in the End or the Nether. There's no day/night cycle, but you can still get lost!

You can also find compasses inside stronghold library chests, or you can buy them from librarian villagers.

In Pocket Edition, maps are made my crafting together nine sheets of paper, and they don't have location markers unless you craft an existing map with a compass.

Clocks aren't generated anywhere in the world, but you can buy them from librarians.

Crafting

YOU CAN HOLD A MAP TO SEE IT FULL SIZE...

...OR PUT IT IN THE OFFHAND SLOT FOR A MINIMAP

LIBRARIANS SELL COMPASSES AND CLOCKS

87

VILLAGE SECRETS

Villages are collections of buildings that can be found in plains, savanna and desert biomes. They make a great place for a base, offering a ready supply of food and villagers to trade with!

THERE'S A WELL AT THE CENTRE OF EVERY VILLAGE

VILLAGES ARE MADE OF "LOCAL" MATERIAL

Villages contain many different buildings, usually constructed from "local" material, such as wood or sandstone:

Wells are the centre of a village. You'll find one in each village.

Huts have a rounded roof and dirt floor. They usually contain one villager, but they may spawn empty.

Small houses have a flat roof (sometimes with a balcony) and a stone floor. They may spawn with a villager attached, but since they have no door they aren't considered homes for individual villagers.

Large houses have triangular roofs and a single large, L-shaped room. They always house two villagers.

Butcher's shops contain a "counter" made of slabs and a fenced-off yard at the rear. The building will always spawn containing a butcher and sometimes a second villager.

Libraries are long, narrow buildings with large windows. They contain tables, bookshelves and a crafting table. The building will always contain one librarian and one other villager.

Blacksmith's have a slabbed roof and large, open porch, with a smelting pool containing lava and two furnaces. They also contain a chest with several common items inside. Blacksmiths spawn with the building, but don't live there.

Churches are large, tall structures with three floors. On the ground floor, you'll find an "altar" made of stairs, and on the second floor, you'll find an outdoor balcony. Churches spawn with one priest and sometimes another villager.

THIS VILLAGE HAS LOTS OF BUILDINGS IN IT!

A PATH THAT GOES OVER WATER TURNS INTO A WALKWAY

Village Secrets

Villages are supposed to have at least one well, one house and one villager, although they can be a lot larger.

You can build new homes in villages – just make sure there's a door within 60 blocks of the village centre and it will be treated as a new home. It may even help a new villager spawn!

Mobs can spawn inside large houses, so add more torches to protect the villagers. Mobs can and will kill villagers, so look after them. They're no good to you dead!

While villagers are normally friendly, attacking one with a tool or weapon can activate the village's iron golem, which will arrive to protect it – by attacking you!

Ravines and caves can sometimes eat into village structures, causing parts of them to disappear. Watch out for these ruined villages because they look great!

Villages are great places to start a base because you'll have a good supply of food nearby and villagers to trade with, as well as access to rare block types like bookshelves. If you're lucky enough to encounter one early on, make use of it!

If you want to make a village your own, then why not fortify it with defensive walls? Keeping mobs out (or even trapping and killing them if they come near!) can be a fun way to learn about making traps and other defences.

Villagers will harvest and replant crops in their farms, so make sure you leave some for them to work with!

SOMETIMES VILLAGES GENERATE WITH PARTIAL BUILDINGS

VILLAGERS WILL HARVEST THEN REPLANT CROPS

89

JUNGLE TEMP

Jungle temples are mostly built of cobblestone and mossy cobblestone, and they only appear in the jungle biome. They're full of hidden treasures just waiting to be looted, but watch out as they're littered with deadly traps and puzzles too!

Jungle temples are large, stone structures that sit in the tops of trees in jungles, although they're often hard to find because a thick cover of leaves and vines tends to block them from view.

The temples have three floors in total, and are mostly built out of cobblestone and moss stone. A puzzle inside will lead you to up to two chests, but you have to get past several traps before you can open them.

The chests inside jungle temples contain random amounts of bone, rotten flesh, gold ingots, iron ingots, diamonds, saddles, emeralds, enchanted books and iron, gold and diamond horse armour. You can also find a dispenser full of arrows to collect!

Jungle temples are one of the few places in the game where mechanisms generate. As well as a huge amount of naturally occurring moss stone (680 blocks), each temple can provide you with a free source of redstone dust (15 pieces), tripwire hooks (4), chiselled stone bricks (3), levers (3), sticky pistons (3), dispensers (2) and redstone repeaters (1).

Unlike desert temples, jungle temples only contain two chests and are a lot harder to find, so they're less valuable to

explorers. If you're trying to discover loot, it makes more sense to look for desert temples, although it's worth pointing out that desert temples are a lot more deadly. If you want to get your loot at a lower risk, jungle temples are the place to go!

JUNGLE TEMPLES CAN BE HIDDEN BY LEAVES

THEY ONLY APPEAR IN THE JUNGLE BIOME

TWO OF THE THREE FLOORS ARE EMPTY

LE SECRETS

Getting in and out of a jungle temple without taking any damage is tricky, but it can still be done. Here's how to get the loot without setting off any of the traps. Make sure you've got a pair of shears handy!

When you find a temple, locate the top of it and enter by breaking a hole in the roof. There are three floors in every jungle temple, and the top two are empty and harmless. Once you're inside, head down the stairs to reach the lowest floor.

At the bottom of the stairs, check whether the levers are on your left or right.

If the levers are on the left, then hit them in this order: right, left, left, right.

If the levers are on the right, use this order: left, right, right, left.

This will open up a secret door revealing a chest, and you're now free to collect the contents within.

There's more! You must continue walking into the temple to find the second chest. Go slowly, keeping a look out for tripwires. You can use shears to safely disarm tripwires and cut away the leaves obscuring traps so that you can see the temple layout properly.

At the end of the hall, you'll find a second chest. Be careful as there's a tripwire directly in front of it, so don't rush to open it until you've cut it with the shears.

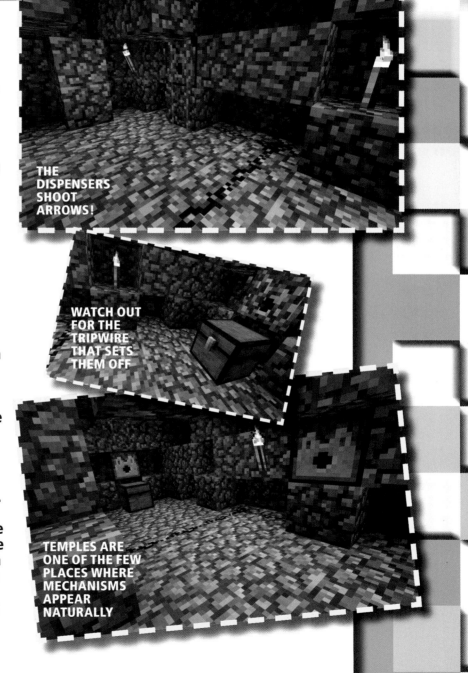

THE DISPENSERS SHOOT ARROWS!

WATCH OUT FOR THE TRIPWIRE THAT SETS THEM OFF

TEMPLES ARE ONE OF THE FEW PLACES WHERE MECHANISMS APPEAR NATURALLY

Once you've disarmed the traps and looted the chests, remember you can also empty the dispensers if you want to for free arrows!

91

DESERT TEMPLE SECRETS

Desert temples appear in desert biomes and can be easily seen from far away. However, they may be partially buried in sand, which can disguise them and make getting inside difficult. Once inside, though, the trick is looting the rare treasures and blocks, then getting out alive!

GET UP HIGH TO SPOT TEMPLES

DESERT TEMPLES MIGHT BE PARTIALLY BURIED IN SAND

Each desert temple hides four treasure chests, but also an explosive trap that can kill you and destroy the chests if you don't take care!

The chests contain bones, rotten flesh, gunpowder, sand, string, spider eyes, enchanted books, saddles, golden apples, gold ingots, iron ingots, emeralds, diamonds, iron, golden or diamond horse armour, and enchanted golden apples. Most of these things are rare, so it's worth the risk!

As well as chests, desert temples contain a few rare blocks that you might want to bring back with you. There's always one block of blue stained clay above the temple's pit, and up to 59 blocks of orange stained clay are used as decoration in the walls and floor. Temples are also a good source of ready-made chiselled sandstone (34 blocks) and smooth sandstone as well (189 blocks).

If you're exploring with a map, desert temples always appear as small, grey blobs. Remember that they may be partially buried, so even if it doesn't look like a temple have a dig around and see what you can find. They all have a hole in the roof, which means it's normally easy to find an entrance even if the door is covered.

YOU CAN GET RARE BLOCKS LIKE STAINED CLAY AND CHISELLED SANDSTONE

THE SYMBOL ON THE GROUND HIDES THE TREASURE

To help you take home the treasures within a desert temple, here's our step-by-step guide to getting in and out of one alive!

■ Be aware that desert temples are built on top of a large pit that contains treasure chests, but also an explosive trap. The pit is found beneath the block of blue clay at the centre of a temple, and the pressure pad that sets off the trap is directly beneath the blue clay at the base of the pit.

■ To get down without setting off the trap, you have to dig your way to the bottom of the temple. Start at the temple doorway, face the blue clay block and dig a stairway down until the staircase breaks into the main pit.

■ Quickly place some torches to light the pit. This will stop monsters spawning and setting off the trap.

■ Carefully make your way to the bottom of the pit. Don't jump!

■ Empty the chests, avoiding the pressure plate. When the chests are empty, head back to the surface.

■ Desert temples are the only place where TNT spawns in the Overworld – there are nine blocks beneath the pit floor. You can only collect TNT if you have a Silk Touch-enchanted pickaxe. If you don't, stay as far away as possible!

IF YOU CAN'T FIND THE ENTRANCE, YOU CAN GET IN UP TOP

BE CAREFUL NOT TO TRIGGER THE TNT!

93

OCEAN MONUMENT SECRETS

Ocean monuments exist only in the Console and PC editions (at time of writing!), and are incredibly difficult to enter and defeat. They generate in deep ocean biomes and are entirely submerged, making it hard to survive inside them, so don't worry if you struggle to beat one!

OCEAN MONUMENTS ARE MADE OUT OF PRISMARINE

ELDER GUARDIANS ARE STRONG AND DEADLY

Ocean monuments are built entirely from prismarine and lit by sea lanterns. Very strong fish-like enemies called guardians spawn in and around them, and attack anything that comes near. Each one also contains three elder guardians, which are even larger and stronger!

The building is made up of a large central section with a random number of smaller rooms off it, held aloft by pillars that stretch down to the ocean floor. In the centre of the main section, you'll find the treasure chamber, which contains eight gold blocks surrounded by dark prismarine. When killed, guardians drop prismarine shards, raw fish, and prismarine crystals. They're also the only place where you can collect sponges.

Defeating an ocean monument and retrieving the treasure requires a lot of equipment, potions and enchantments, and is difficult to do until late in the game. Your chances of living will be improved if your armour has enchantments like Respiration, Aqua Affinity and Depth Strider, but if you're missing any of those you can get the same effects by bringing Potions of Water Breathing (so you don't drown), a Potion of Night Vision (so you can see clearly underwater) and a Potion of Speed (so you can walk fast underwater) to use instead.

GUARDIANS WILL ZAP ANYTHING – EVEN SQUID

OCEAN LANTERNS LIGHT UP TEMPLES

THE TREASURE CHAMBER

BREAK THE TREASURE CHAMBER TO FIND GOLD BLOCKS

Survival Tactics

Surviving inside an ocean monument is already difficult enough even with mobs turned off, so don't go near one unless you have strong equipment, and don't take anything unnecessary. If you die inside one, it's almost impossible to get your stuff back before it disappears!

Getting past the guardians to enter a monument in the first place can be difficult. Invisibility potions and ender pearls make it a lot easier to get past them though, but you can't avoid a fight entirely if you try to enter underwater.

One way you can avoid a fight is to use cobblestone to build an "airlock", then tunnel down into the monument, extending a ladder downwards. This removes water as you go and lets you build a cobblestone shield around yourself at each step. Guardians can't attack through solid blocks, and you can kill them more easily if they're directly beneath you.

Fighting an elder guardian gives you a Mining Fatigue status effect, so you can't mine your way out. For this reason, it helps to have an escape route ready made before you approach the treasure chamber.

To make it easier to find and complete a monument, you may want to build an underwater base nearby. Place a bed in there to reset your spawn point in case you die in the temple, and leave an ender chest inside so it's easy to supply yourself with potions, food and equipment backups in advance.

ABANDONED MINE SECRETS

Abandoned mines are generated naturally in the Overworld. You usually find them deep underground, but they're sometimes near the floor of shallow oceans. They're full of items and enemies, making them great places to explore and build experience without too much danger!

THE STARTING ROOM OF A MINE

MINES CAN INTERSECT NATURAL CAVES

The start of a mine is always a large room with a flat floor that's covered in dirt, with up to four exits. There are 3x3 mineshafts extending out of this room, then more mineshafts leading off those to form a maze of mineshafts.

Mineshafts may intersect with natural caves, so you don't always enter at the "start", and the layout is random, so you never know what you'll find! Staircases and intersections allow you to move up or down a level, but there isn't always any logic.

It's possible for two mines to generate near one another and interconnect, allowing huge structures to form. Exploring them can take a lot of time, so don't get lost!

Corridors contain supports made from oak fences and oak wood planks (often lit by torches). You'll also find rail tracks, minecarts, storage minecarts and cave spider spawners surrounded by cobwebs.

Any storage minecarts can contain rails, torches, bread, name tags, coal, beetroot/melon/pumpkin seeds, iron/gold ingots, golden apples, activator/detector/powered rails, lapis lazuli, redstone, enchanted books/golden apples, diamonds and iron pickaxes.

CORRIDORS INTERSECT AND OVERLAP

THERE'S A SPIDER SPAWNER IN HERE SOMEWHERE!

SPIDERS CAN CREEP UP ON YOU FROM ANY DIRECTION

LOOK OUT FOR MINECARTS!

Survival Tactics

Mines are filled with common enemies like creepers, zombies and skeletons, but their narrow shafts make it easy to fight them off with a sword or bow. There isn't room for them to dodge your attacks or sneak up on you!

The most difficult enemy to fight in mineshafts are cave spiders, because they can attack from almost any direction. It's common to find mineshafts full of spiders and spiderwebs, so bring a pair of shears. You can cut spider webs, allowing you to collect either a web (if you use shears) or string (if you use a sword).

You can identify a cave spider monster spawner from the large amount of cobwebs around them. Using shears or a sword to cut away the webbing is the quickest way to get close enough to break the spawning block, although you can also use water or fire to get rid of the web.

Don't try to use minecarts to ride the rails of mineshafts as the stretches are very short and usually broken. Mineshafts are great places for collecting rails, but they don't lead anywhere interesting when you find them. Pick up the tracks and reuse them yourself later on.

Mineshafts are a good source of wooden planks, which can be useful if you need to craft but don't want to return to the surface. There's almost no other way to get wood underground, unless you can grow a tree there, which takes a long time!

STRONGHOLD SECRETS

Strongholds are large dungeons that spawn underground and it's very difficult to find one just by luck. Most importantly, they're the only way you can reach the End and face the ultimate Minecraft challenge: fighting the ender dragon!

THE THREE MAIN TYPES OF STONE BRICKS IN A STRONGHOLD

STRONGHOLDS ARE FULL OF BOOKS

Strongholds are found deep underground, only appearing 600-1000 blocks away from the spawn point. At present, most versions of Minecraft contain different numbers of strongholds: one (Console), three (Pocket) or 128 (PC).

Luckily, it's possible to find strongholds by using an eye of ender to show you the way. To create an eye of ender, combine an ender pearl (which is dropped when you kill an enderman, or traded with villagers) with blaze powder (which can be created using blaze rods, which are dropped by blazes in the Nether). When you have several eyes of ender, you can start searching.

If you throw an eye of ender, it will move in the direction of the nearest stronghold. You can follow the trail it leaves to recollect the fallen eye, but take care as there's a one-in-five chance of the eye shattering! This is why you need lots before you start. Eventually, you'll locate the right spot on the surface to start digging down, which will lead you to the stronghold's entrance.

Strongholds have multiple floors and huge numbers of rooms in a complicated layout with repeating features, such as stairwells, corridors, jail cells and fountains. Strongholds often have libraries and store rooms, which are good places to find chests and bookshelves when underground.

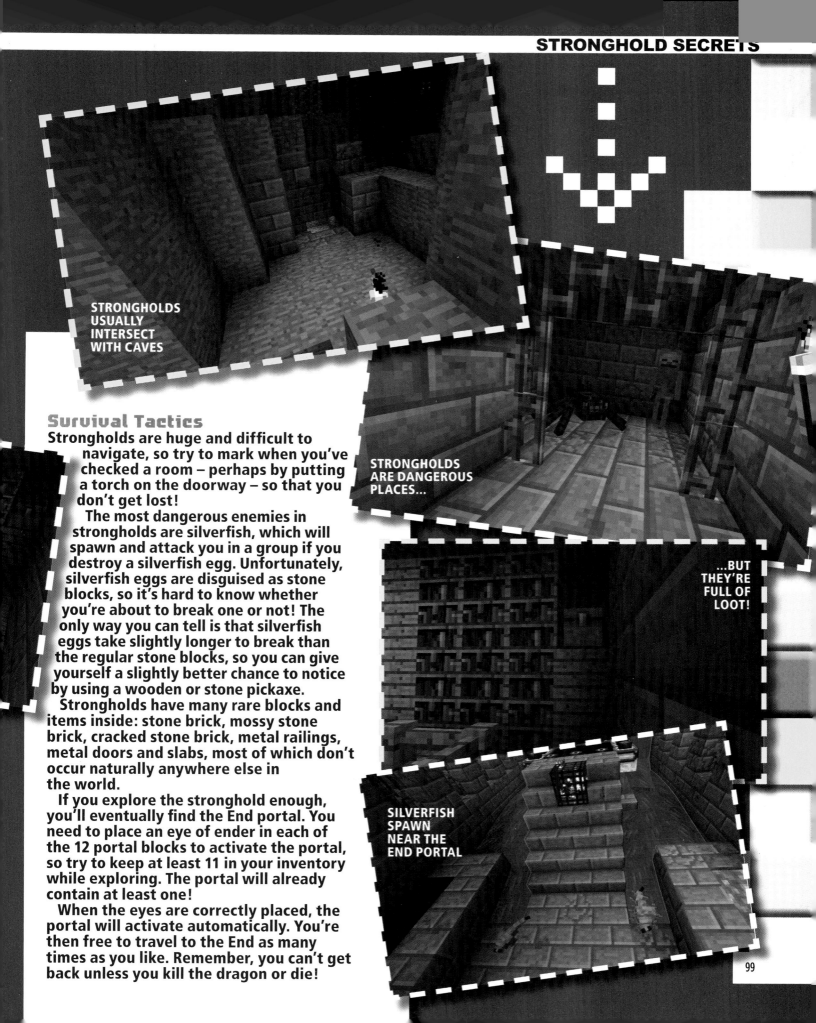

STRONGHOLDS USUALLY INTERSECT WITH CAVES

STRONGHOLDS ARE DANGEROUS PLACES...

...BUT THEY'RE FULL OF LOOT!

SILVERFISH SPAWN NEAR THE END PORTAL

Survival Tactics

Strongholds are huge and difficult to navigate, so try to mark when you've checked a room – perhaps by putting a torch on the doorway – so that you don't get lost!

The most dangerous enemies in strongholds are silverfish, which will spawn and attack you in a group if you destroy a silverfish egg. Unfortunately, silverfish eggs are disguised as stone blocks, so it's hard to know whether you're about to break one or not! The only way you can tell is that silverfish eggs take slightly longer to break than the regular stone blocks, so you can give yourself a slightly better chance to notice by using a wooden or stone pickaxe.

Strongholds have many rare blocks and items inside: stone brick, mossy stone brick, cracked stone brick, metal railings, metal doors and slabs, most of which don't occur naturally anywhere else in the world.

If you explore the stronghold enough, you'll eventually find the End portal. You need to place an eye of ender in each of the 12 portal blocks to activate the portal, so try to keep at least 11 in your inventory while exploring. The portal will already contain at least one!

When the eyes are correctly placed, the portal will activate automatically. You're then free to travel to the End as many times as you like. Remember, you can't get back unless you kill the dragon or die!

IGLOO SECRETS

Igloos are structures that generate in ice plains and cold taiga biomes, with an exterior consisting of snow and ice blocks. They're relatively rare in the game also and hard to spot because they blend into their surroundings, but they're useful!

Inside an igloo, you'll find a redstone torch (giving off light that won't melt snow!), a furnace, bed and crafting table, as well as a carpet made out of white and light grey carpet tiles.

Half of all igloos have a secret basement beneath them, but the only way to tell is to pull up the carpet and search for the trapdoor. You should find the entrance directly opposite the main door, a couple of spaces away from the back wall.

The trapdoor leads to a basement containing a brewing stand, cauldron, chest, priest villager and a zombie villager, as well as everything you need to cure the zombie villager, such as a splash potion of weakness and a golden apple.

IGLOOS ARE MADE OF PACKED SNOW

INSIDE AN IGLOO – THE COOLEST BASE AROUND!

NOT ALL IGLOOS HAVE BASEMENTS

Igloo Secrets

Igloos are the only place you can find beds and brewing stands being generated in the Overworld, so they're very useful, especially if you start in a snowy biome where there may not be any sheep nearby!

The chest always contains a golden apple, coal, apple, wheat, gold nuggets, rotten flesh, stone axes and emeralds.

Watch out as the stone brick walls of an igloo's basement can contain silverfish!

RARE STRUCTURES

Witch Huts

Witch huts only generate in swamp biomes, sometimes on dry ground and sometimes in shallow water. They're always on tall stilts that extend all the way to the ground, and can only be reached by building your way up to the entrance.

Inside, you'll find a few rare items. They're the only place you can scavenge a flower pot and they also contain a cauldron. In the Pocket Edition, the cauldron contains a random potion, and the flower pot has a red mushroom planted in it, so expect to see those in future editions on other platforms!

WITCH HUTS ONLY APPEAR IN SWAMPS

Desert Wells

Wells are very rare structures made of sandstone and slabs that appear in deserts. They're different to wells you find in villages in that they contain less water and don't have any other structures attached, but if you're stuck in a desert and need water they do contain an infinite source! If you're planning to start a base in a desert biome, they're a good excuse to start building in a particular place.

DESERT WELLS AREN'T MUCH USE!

DUNGEONS CONTAIN MONSTER SPAWNERS, SO WATCH OUT!

Dungeons

Dungeons are underground rooms made of cobblestone and moss stone that contain a monster spawner (zombie, skeleton or spider) and up to two chests.

They're always connected to caverns, so you can find them without digging. Their chests contain lots of rare loot, most notably two music discs (13 and Cat).

THE NETHER

The Nether is a weird, alternate dimension full of strong enemies, fire, and lava, but also rare blocks and items to collect. If you want to beat strongholds, visit the End, defeat ocean temples and kill the wither, you must first visit the Nether to get experience and special items!

REACHING THE NETHER

Getting to the Nether means building a Nether portal. First, you need to make a portal frame out of obsidian, which forms where water flows over lava. You can only mine it using a diamond pickaxe! The standard portal size is 4x6 blocks, but if you miss off the corners you can build one using just 10 pieces of obsidian.

When a portal frame is built, you have to set it on fire to activate it. The easiest way to do this is with a flint and steel. When you enter the portal, it will generate a corresponding portal in the Nether, and if you build one in the Nether it will do the same in the Overworld. Almost any mob or entity can use the portal – you can even build minecart rails that travel through it!

TERRAIN

The Nether is mostly composed of Netherrack, a weird, red form of stone that mines very quickly. If you set it on fire, it burns forever. You'll also find soul sand, a sticky type of dirt that causes players and mobs to slow down when they walk over it; glowstone, a light-emitting crystal that hangs from ceilings and shatters into glowstone dust; and Nether quartz ore, which drops Nether quartz when mined and can be crafted into marble.

YOU NEED AN OBSIDIAN PORTAL TO REACH THE NETHER

PORTALS CAN BE SMALL OR LARGE

THE NETHER IS A STRANGE PLACE

EXPLAINED

THE NETHER SECRETS

The Nether has no day/night cycle – compasses and clocks don't work, and will spin unpredictably and uselessly.

Maps created in the Nether don't show the terrain, just a brownish mess. You can still use them to get a rough idea of where you are, but your position indicator will also spin randomly.

When in single-player mode, entering the Nether causes time to freeze in the Overworld, and vice versa.

Lava flows further and more quickly in the Nether.

Meanwhile, water will evaporate the moment it's placed, even if you melt it from ice blocks. Also, snow golems can't survive in the Nether.

If you try and sleep in a bed, it will explode, injuring you. This prevents you from getting stuck in the Nether when you die and potentially being trapped if your portal is damaged.

You can grow trees in the Nether if you bring dirt from the Overworld and give them enough space and light, but their leaves will be brown and dry. If you place a grass block, it will have the same dry, brownish look to it.

Chickens are the only non-hostile mob that can spawn in the Nether. The reason for that is because baby zombie pigmen have a small chance of spawning as chicken jockeys. The only other mob you can find in both the Overworld and the Nether are skeletons, which appear in Nether fortresses.

THERE IS FOOD IN THE NETHER – AS LONG AS YOU LIKE MUSHROOMS!

PORTALS APPEAR IN THE NETHER WHEN YOU USE THEM IN THE OVERWORLD

A WITHER SKELETON AND A REGULAR SKELETON

You can find red and brown mushrooms growing all over the Nether, but the only other naturally occurring plant is Nether wart.

NETHER FORTRESSES

If you visit the Nether, you'll eventually encounter large castles and walkways positioned high above the lava lakes. These are Nether fortresses, the only structures to generate naturally in the Nether.

NETHER
FORTRESSES ARE
FULL OF WALKWAYS

WITHER SKELETONS
ARE COMMON IN
FORTRESSES

Nether fortresses are made entirely of Nether bricks, which exist as Nether brick blocks, Nether brick fences and Nether brick stairs. You can smelt Netherrack to craft Nether bricks, but they can also be collected from Nether fortresses.

Players must visit a Nether fortress at least once to brew potions, because they're the only place in the game where you can collect Nether wart, which is the basis of almost all useful potions. If you haven't yet found a brewing stand, you can also collect blaze rods from blazes (which only spawn in fortresses) so that you can craft one.

Nether fortresses are the only place in the Nether where you can find chests. They mostly contain items that are easily obtained in the Overworld, such as armour, ingots, diamonds and saddles, but they also contain Nether wart (which is useful because not all fortresses have naturally growing Nether wart), and both obsidian and a flint and steel, which can help you rebuild and reactivate a portal if you get stuck in the Nether.

Wither skeletons are only found in Nether fortresses, which is important because to summon the wither you need three wither skeleton skulls. You have to kill a lot of skeletons to get them, as wither skulls only drop around one in every 40 kills!

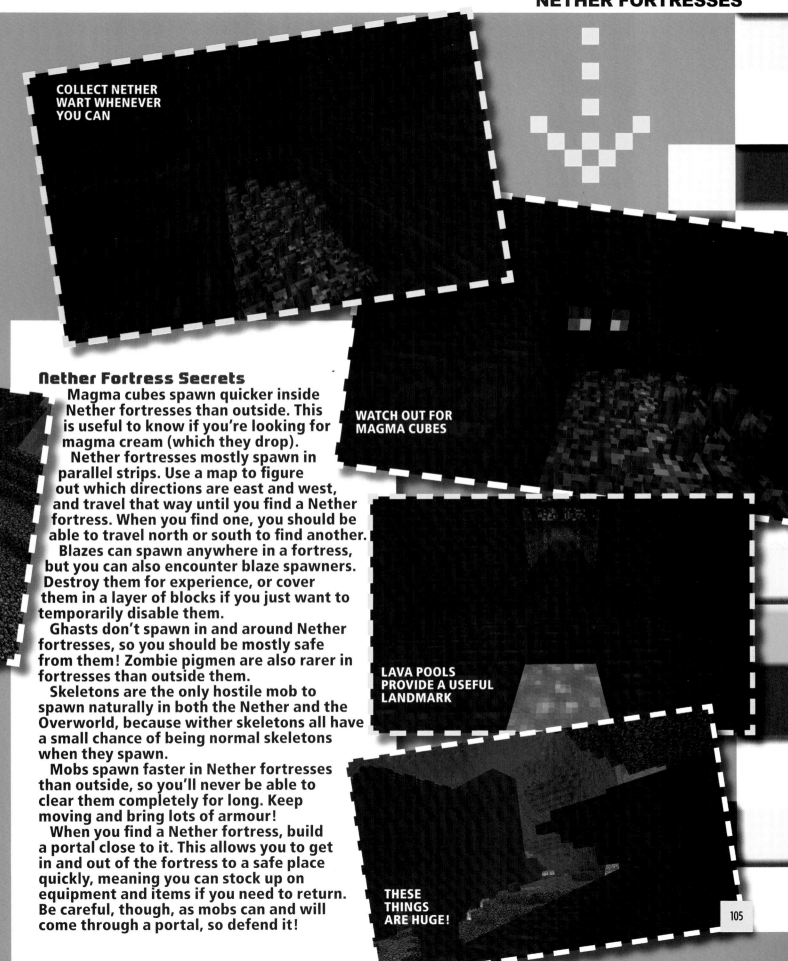

COLLECT NETHER WART WHENEVER YOU CAN

WATCH OUT FOR MAGMA CUBES

Nether Fortress Secrets

Magma cubes spawn quicker inside Nether fortresses than outside. This is useful to know if you're looking for magma cream (which they drop).

Nether fortresses mostly spawn in parallel strips. Use a map to figure out which directions are east and west, and travel that way until you find a Nether fortress. When you find one, you should be able to travel north or south to find another.

Blazes can spawn anywhere in a fortress, but you can also encounter blaze spawners. Destroy them for experience, or cover them in a layer of blocks if you just want to temporarily disable them.

Ghasts don't spawn in and around Nether fortresses, so you should be mostly safe from them! Zombie pigmen are also rarer in fortresses than outside them.

Skeletons are the only hostile mob to spawn naturally in both the Nether and the Overworld, because wither skeletons all have a small chance of being normal skeletons when they spawn.

Mobs spawn faster in Nether fortresses than outside, so you'll never be able to clear them completely for long. Keep moving and bring lots of armour!

When you find a Nether fortress, build a portal close to it. This allows you to get in and out of the fortress to a safe place quickly, meaning you can stock up on equipment and items if you need to return. Be careful, though, as mobs can and will come through a portal, so defend it!

LAVA POOLS PROVIDE A USEFUL LANDMARK

THESE THINGS ARE HUGE!

REACHING
THE END

The End is the third and (so far!) final dimension within Minecraft, separate from the Overworld and the Nether. It's the home of the ender dragon, Minecraft's "boss", but beating the dragon is just your ticket to exploring even more of this mysterious world.

THE JOURNEY TO THE END STARTS BY REACHING THE NETHER

KILL BLAZES TO GET BLAZE RODS

How To Visit The End

If you want to beat the game, here's how to get to the End. There are other ways to fulfil certain tasks, like trading with villagers, but this is one definite path to success:

■ Collect resources until you can craft a diamond pickaxe. You'll need ender pearls later on, so try to kill endermen as often as possible.

■ Mine obsidian using your diamond pickaxe, then use it to create a Nether portal.

■ Enter the Nether and look for a Nether fortress. Kill blazes to collect the blaze rods they drop. You need six. The more you have, the better the chance of success.

■ Return to the Overworld. Craft blaze rods into blaze powder. Combine the powder with ender pearls to create as many eyes of ender as possible. You need a minimum of 11, but - unsurprisingly - the more of them you have the better, as they break easily.

■ Use your eyes of ender to locate the nearest stronghold and travel there. Explore the stronghold until you find the End portal inside.

■ Activate the portal by placing eyes of ender in the 12 End portal blocks around it.

■ You may now enter the portal to the End!

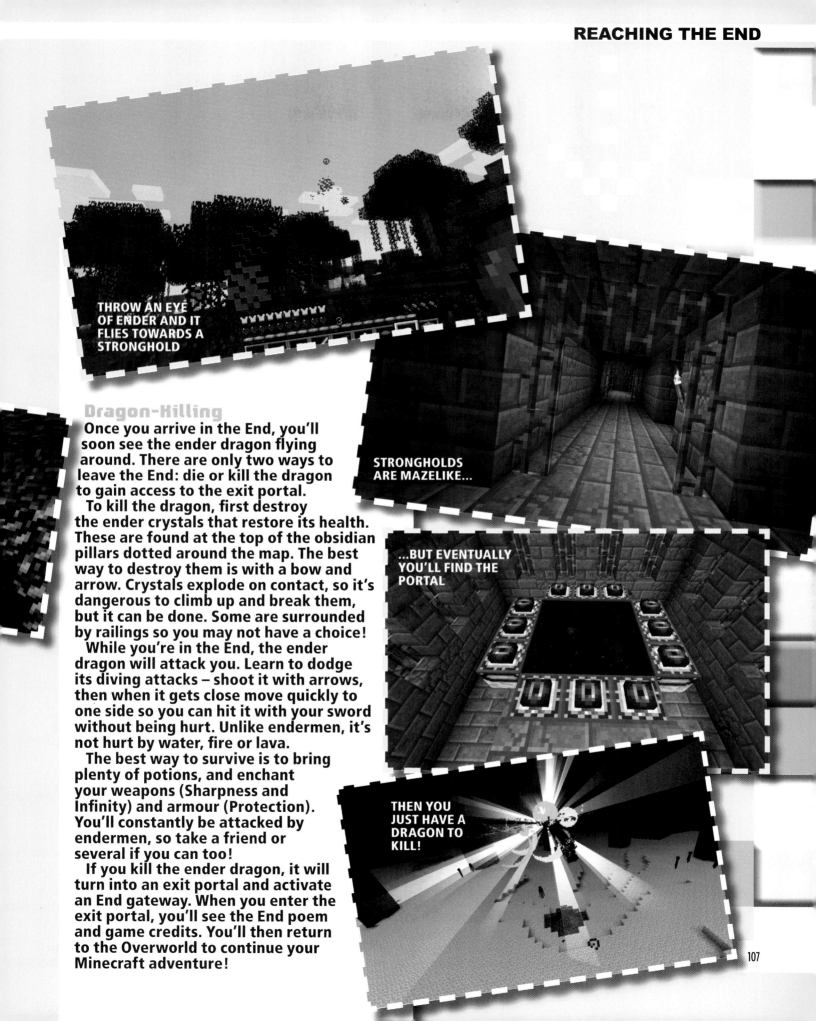

THROW AN EYE OF ENDER AND IT FLIES TOWARDS A STRONGHOLD

STRONGHOLDS ARE MAZELIKE...

...BUT EVENTUALLY YOU'LL FIND THE PORTAL

THEN YOU JUST HAVE A DRAGON TO KILL!

Dragon-Killing

Once you arrive in the End, you'll soon see the ender dragon flying around. There are only two ways to leave the End: die or kill the dragon to gain access to the exit portal.

To kill the dragon, first destroy the ender crystals that restore its health. These are found at the top of the obsidian pillars dotted around the map. The best way to destroy them is with a bow and arrow. Crystals explode on contact, so it's dangerous to climb up and break them, but it can be done. Some are surrounded by railings so you may not have a choice!

While you're in the End, the ender dragon will attack you. Learn to dodge its diving attacks – shoot it with arrows, then when it gets close move quickly to one side so you can hit it with your sword without being hurt. Unlike endermen, it's not hurt by water, fire or lava.

The best way to survive is to bring plenty of potions, and enchant your weapons (Sharpness and Infinity) and armour (Protection). You'll constantly be attacked by endermen, so take a friend or several if you can too!

If you kill the ender dragon, it will turn into an exit portal and activate an End gateway. When you enter the exit portal, you'll see the End poem and game credits. You'll then return to the Overworld to continue your Minecraft adventure!

107

GUIDE TO THE END

The End is a stark and mostly empty dimension that's home to endermen and the ender dragon. If you explore for long enough, eventually you should find an End city, which is your reward for persevering. Here, you can collect some of the rarest items in the game!

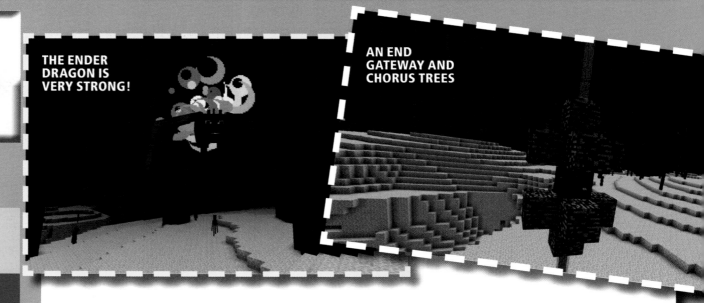

THE ENDER DRAGON IS VERY STRONG!

AN END GATEWAY AND CHORUS TREES

When you arrive in the End in Minecraft, you will appear on a large island (the central island) full of obsidian pillars, which is where the ender dragon lives. Once you've defeated the ender dragon, you can then gain access to the exit portal (which returns you to the Overworld) and End gateways, which in turn allow you to reach the rest of the End easily.

To use an End gateway (which is a small portal surrounded by bedrock), you have to throw an ender pearl at it. This will then teleport you to one of the other islands in the End so that you can explore the world further.

TERRAIN

The End consists of floating islands above a lethal void. The islands are made of End stone, a rare form of stone that has high blast resistance and can't be picked up by endermen.

On the outer islands, you can find forests of chorus trees. These are thin, jagged plants, that can be broken with any tool, causing them to drop up to one chorus fruit. At the end of their "branches", they also generate chorus flowers, which can be mined and planted in End stone to grow another chorus tree.

The outer islands stretch far in every direction without any real features other than chorus trees until you find an End city.

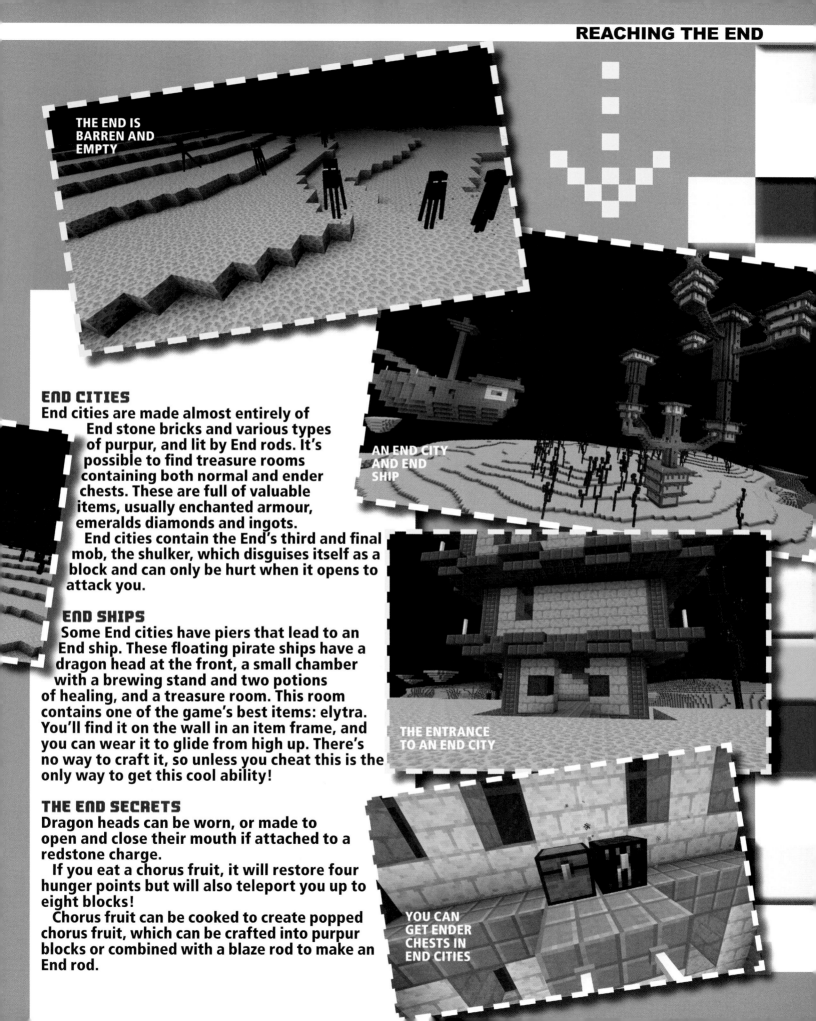

THE END IS
BARREN AND
EMPTY

AN END CITY
AND END
SHIP

END CITIES

End cities are made almost entirely of
End stone bricks and various types
of purpur, and lit by End rods. It's
possible to find treasure rooms
containing both normal and ender
chests. These are full of valuable
items, usually enchanted armour,
emeralds diamonds and ingots.
End cities contain the End's third and final
mob, the shulker, which disguises itself as a
block and can only be hurt when it opens to
attack you.

END SHIPS

Some End cities have piers that lead to an
End ship. These floating pirate ships have a
dragon head at the front, a small chamber
with a brewing stand and two potions
of healing, and a treasure room. This room
contains one of the game's best items: elytra.
You'll find it on the wall in an item frame, and
you can wear it to glide from high up. There's
no way to craft it, so unless you cheat this is the
only way to get this cool ability!

THE ENTRANCE
TO AN END CITY

THE END SECRETS

Dragon heads can be worn, or made to
open and close their mouth if attached to a
redstone charge.
If you eat a chorus fruit, it will restore four
hunger points but will also teleport you up to
eight blocks!
Chorus fruit can be cooked to create popped
chorus fruit, which can be crafted into purpur
blocks or combined with a blaze rod to make an
End rod.

YOU CAN
GET ENDER
CHESTS IN
END CITIES

ADVANCED SECRETS

Become An Expert!

Across the 100+ pages of this guide so far, we've gone right through the breadth of the Minecraft game and come up with no shortage of tips along the way. This chapter, though, is for those who want to take even more adventurous steps forward, and who want to become Minecraft experts! Step this way, then, if you want to make the game even tougher, if you fancy discovering secret mobs, and if you want to uncover the mysteries of uncraftable items!

TRADING WITH VILLAGERS

One way to get hold of rare and hard-to-find items is to trade with villagers. You can trade with any villager you haven't attacked or angered, and the more you trade the better your reputation becomes, giving you access to superior or cheaper items!

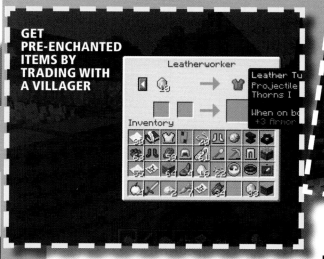

GET PRE-ENCHANTED ITEMS BY TRADING WITH A VILLAGER

FARMERS MOSTLY SELL FOOD

The currency for trading is emeralds, which you can collect from chests or mine in the extreme hills biome. You can also sell items to villagers to get some emeralds.

To trade with a villager, walk up to them and press the "use" button. The trading screen will appear, allowing you to offer your items. If the villager accepts your offer, they'll show you goods in return. You're then free to complete or reject the trade by taking the item or emeralds on offer.

Villagers

Villagers have one of 11 professions, grouped by five different clothing colours. On the trading screen, you can see which type of villager you're trading with.

Farmers (brown robes)

Standard farmers buy large amounts of raw food (wheat, potatoes, carrots) and sell cooked and crafted food back to you.

Fishermen sell enchanted rods, and buy lots of string (15-20 pieces) and coal (16-24 pieces). If you give them fish and an emerald, they return cooked fish.

Shepherds buy large amounts of wool (16-22 blocks) and sell shears and coloured wool.

Fletchers buy string (15-20 pieces) and sell bows and arrows. You can sell gravel and an emerald for flints to use as arrowheads.

TRADING WITH A VILLAGER MAKES THEM HEAL

Librarians (white robes)

Librarians buy large amounts of paper (24-36 sheets) and books (8-10 copies), and they also sell enchanted books, compasses, bookshelves and more. If your reputation is high enough, you can buy name tags off librarians for 20-22 emeralds.

LIBRARIANS CAN SELL ENCHANTED BOOKS

Blacksmiths (black aprons)

Armorers buy coal (16-24 pieces), iron ingots and diamonds. They sell armour, including chainmail armour, which is impossible to craft.

Weapon smiths buy coal (16-24 pieces), iron ingots and diamonds. They then sell iron axes and swords, which are enchanted and are even made of diamond at higher reputation levels.

Tool smiths buy coal (16-24 blocks), iron ingots and diamonds. They sell enchanted iron shovels/pickaxes, and at higher levels enchanted diamond pickaxes.

SOME VILLAGERS WEAR APRONS, LIKE THIS BUTCHER

Butchers (white aprons)

Standard butchers will buy raw meat (14-18 chickens or porkchops) and coal (16-24 pieces). They sell cooked porkchops and roast chickens.

Leatherworkers buy leather (9-12 pieces) and sell leather armour and saddles.

Priests (purple robes)

There's only one profession for priest villagers: cleric. They buy rotten flesh (36-40 pieces) and gold ingots (8-10 bars). They sell redstone dust, lapis lazuli and glowstone, but at high reputations also ender pearls and bottle o' enchanting!

CLERICS HAVE THE RAREST ITEMS

113

VILLAGER SECRETS

Villagers aren't just good for trading – there are lots of other things about them that make Minecraft more fun to play!

VILLAGERS ONLY DESPAWN IF THEY DIE

VILLAGERS CAN BREED TO REPLACE DEAD ONES

Villager Behaviour

Unlike other mobs, villagers will never despawn. Once they appear in your world, they can only disappear if they die. They spawn inside empty houses, and it's possible to add houses to villages to encourage new villagers to spawn. The game determines how many empty houses there are by the number of valid doors added within the scope of the village. Valid doors are counted as any with more "outside" space in front of than behind. Outside space is any block with nothing but sky above it.

Villagers can also breed to replace any villagers who've died, and baby villagers will grow up after 20 minutes. The type of villager they breed is random and doesn't depend on their profession.

Villagers have eight inventory slots, which the player can't currently access, but can help fill by throwing items. They'll only collect bread, carrots, potatoes, wheat and seeds, but they can hold full stacks of each, which means they can sometimes collect food you'd have otherwise kept for yourself. If villagers have a lot of food, they'll share it with other villagers, and will only breed if they have a lot of food.

Any brown-robed villager will tend to crops (wheat, potatoes and carrots) planted inside the village. If they don't have enough food, they'll harvest the crops then plant replacements. This means you can often find well-stocked farms in villages.

VILLAGERS
HARVEST CROPS
ON THEIR OWN

Enemy Villagers

If a zombie attacks a villager, it has a chance of turning it into a zombie villager. This chance depends on the difficulty level: 0% on Easy, 50% on Normal and 100% on Hard. Children can also be turned into baby zombies, which are much stronger and harder to kill than fully grown zombies.

KEEP ZOMBIES
AWAY FROM
VILLAGERS OR THEY
MIGHT TURN

In the same way that lightning strikes can transform creepers and pigs into charged creepers and zombie pigmen, if a lightning bolt strikes close enough to a villager (within 3-4 blocks of where they're standing) the villager will turn into a witch. You can't turn a witch back into a villager, so kill it before it does too much damage!

Killing friendly villagers has no positive effect. They don't drop anything and it will lower your reputation with other villagers so they might refuse to trade with you. The village's iron golem might also come and attack you for harming its masters, which means a difficult fight for very little reward.

IRON GOLEMS
PROTECT LARGER
VILLAGES

Villager Secrets

Villagers will run indoors at night – they know better than to hang around waiting for hostile mobs to turn up!

Villagers can still see invisible players, so don't think you can sneak past them with a potion!

Unlike most mobs, villagers are smart enough to open and close doors. If you want to keep them out, use a steel door.

The only place you can find a villager outside a village is in an Igloo basement, where a priest villager has been captured.

VILLAGERS
WILL RUN
INDOORS AT
NIGHT

115

ELYTRA

Ever wondering what it must feel like to be a bird gliding above the trees and viewing the terrain below? Well, now you can find out for yourself with this awesome pair of wings!

ELYTRA ARE ONLY FOUND ON END SHIPS

ELYTRA FOLD ONTO YOUR BACK LIKE A CAPE

GLIDING ON ELYTRA

If you manage to reach the End, defeat the ender dragon and survive long enough to find an End city with an End ship, your reward – assuming you look in the right place (an item frame on the treasure chamber's wall) – is a pair of elytra. They're one of the hardest items to find in the game, but also one of the most fun!

Elytra are wings that allow you to glide when you jump from a high place. You equip them as an armour chestpiece, so you can be vulnerable while wearing them, but the trade-off is that you're a lot harder to hit when you're flying through the air!

To activate the elytra, press and hold the jump button in mid-air. While in flight, the elytra will slowly lose durability. A standard pair has seven minutes of flight in them, and they can be enchanted with Unbreaking to give up to 71 minutes of flight for a single pair!

When the elytra's durability runs out, they don't break completely but can't be used to glide until they're repaired. You can repair them by crafting two pairs together on a crafting grid, or applying leather using an anvil. You need four leather to repair them completely.

While you're wearing elytra, it's almost impossible to take fall damage, unless you stall while gliding.

In case you're wondering, the elytra's name comes from the hardened forewings found on beetles and earwigs. In real life, they aren't used for flying, only for protecting the actual wings.

MINECRAFT NIGHTS

Every Minecraft player knows that the night is an integral part of the game. When the sun sets, you have to change everything you're doing to stay alive. But there's more going on than just mobs coming out…

NIGHT SECRETS

Night begins when the sun has completely disappeared below the horizon, which is also the point where you're allowed to sleep in a bed. It takes 20 minutes for the entire day/night cycle to run in Minecraft. Daytime lasts for 10 minutes, sunset and sunrise last for 90 seconds each, and the dangerous, mob-spawning part of night runs for seven minutes in total.

The moon is only visible at night and changes every time it goes through a cycle. Like real life, the moon has eight different phases.

The phase of the moon has a number of effects on how mobs behave. The more full the moon is, the higher the chance of a skeleton or zombie picking up a weapon or armour, spawning with a weapon or armour, and having weapons and armour that are enchanted. If you're playing on Hard (or Hardcore) difficult mode, a fuller moon also means that spiders have a greater chance of spawning with a status effect such as Speed that makes them stronger.

There's only one time you can sleep in a bed when it isn't night, and that's during a storm. When you wake up, the storm will have passed and the rain will be gone, so it's a good way to prevent lightning damaging your buildings!

MOON PHASES

A FULL MOON MAKES SLIMES MORE LIKELY

FULL MOONS RAISE THE CHANCE OF EQUIPPED MOBS SPAWNING

MOBS SPAWN WHEN THE SKY GOES FULLY DARK

117

MAKE MINECRAFT HARDER

If you've been playing Minecraft a long time and are finding it quite easy, there are a few things you can do to make the game harder. Here are our suggestions for ways advanced players can try out something new!

YOU DON'T WANT TO SEE THIS SCREEN IN HARDCORE MODE

Game over!

Score: 0

You cannot respawn in hardcore mode!

Delete world

AN ABANDONED MINESHAFT BECOMES AN ESSENTIAL SOURCE OF WOOD

Play in Hardcore mode.

Hardcore mode is the most difficult way to play Minecraft because you only get one chance – and when we say that, we really mean it! Most of the game's attributes (like hunger deterioration and mob health levels) are the same as Hard mode, which means that they're a constant source of danger to you. But in Hardcore mode, you only have one life, and if you lose it the world you're playing in is locked forever. That's certainly an incentive to play it safe!

If you like, you could keep a note of the world seed and try again and again to beat your previous survival time. Maybe even challenge your friends to survive longer than you did!

Become a Moleman or Molewoman

Many people try to spend as little time underground as possible, because it's dangerous, claustrophobic and full of mobs. If you want a challenge, you should embrace the subterranean lifestyle. Go underground as soon as you start the game and try to never return to the surface again!

This challenge is difficult, especially when you start to get low on wood, but it's far from impossible. If you like, you can play a variant where you're only allowed overground at night. If it's good enough for mobs to be out in the dark, it's good enough for the Mole People!

THE BATS WILL BE YOUR ONLY FRIENDS UNDERGROUND

Don't Ever Build

Building is a major part of Minecraft, so try and play the game without building anything! Adventure mode makes it impossible to place or destroy blocks, but that's designed for worlds where someone has already given you the items you need. This relies on you not breaking your own rules, though you can set them yourself when you start!

Under the rules of this challenge, "not building" means you can't place any block that isn't furniture or food, so beds, cakes, crops and crafting tables are fine, but stone, wood, stairs and iron blocks aren't. We recommend you find a village to move into, but you could also hollow out a den. Either way, it will definitely make the game much harder.

WHEN YOU CAN'T BUILD, VILLAGES ARE VERY USEFUL!

KEEP MOVING AND YOU'RE MORE LIKELY TO SEE WEIRD THINGS, LIKE THIS HORSE-SHAPED CLIFF

Keep Wandering

Embrace the life of a nomad: pick a direction, keep walking and don't turn back. With limited space to carry goods, you'll have to make some hard choices about what's most useful for you now versus what might be useful in the future.

The rule is that you can never return to a bed you've already slept in (unless you die) and that you have to end every day out of sight of wherever you started it.

A DONKEY OR MULE MEANS EXTRA INVENTORY SPACE IN NOMADIC PLAY

EVERY MOB SECRET

Every mob in Minecraft hides a secret. It might be behaviour, it might be a drop or it might be something special they can do. We've found out every mob secret so you don't have to!

Chickens are the only mob that can be bred in two different ways: by hatching out of a thrown egg or if the player feeds them seeds.

Cows give milk if you use a bucket on them. Milk can cure status effects no matter where they came from and be crafted into food.

Mooshrooms can drop their mushrooms and turn into a regular cow if you use shears on them. You can also use a bowl on a mooshroom to get mushroom stew.

Pigs can be ridden using saddles even without being tamed, and transform into zombie pigmen if they get struck by lightning!

Rabbits have different skins to match which biome they spawn in. Rabbits with white hides appear in snowy biomes, for instance.

Sheep can be dyed different colours and regrow their wool by eating grass.

Squid drop ink sacs, which are the only mob drop that can be used as dye.

Ocelots are the only mob that scare away creepers. They also change skin when tamed.

Horses & Donkeys can breed with another species. Breeding a horse and donkey creates a mule!

Wolves, when tamed, wear collars, which you can then dye any colour.

Cave Spiders are the only mob that can poison you.

Endermen can pick up and move blocks, and (in the latest version) they're the only mob to appear in all three realms: the Overworld, the Nether and the End.

Spiders are the only mob that can climb walls. In Pocket Edition, they can also spawn from leaves.

Zombie Pigmen, although normally restricted to the Nether, can spawn in Overworld if a Nether portal is nearby.

Blazes are the only mobs that take damage from snowballs.

Creepers turn into charged creepers when struck by lightning.

Elder Guardians drop sponges when killed by the player, and inflict the Mining Fatigue status effect.

Endermites get killed by endermen if they appear after teleporting.

Ghasts have the longest range of all normal mobs – they can attack you from 100 blocks away.

Guardians can fire a laser beam that can't be dodged.

Magma Cubes spawn more frequently in Nether fortresses compared to the rest of the Nether.

Shulkers are only found in the End, and camouflage themselves as blocks when closed. They appear even in Peaceful mode.

Silverfish can hide inside certain types of block in order to regain their health.

Skeletons can make creepers drop a music disc if they shoot and kill one with their arrows.

Slimes will spawn more frequently if there's a full moon.

Witches are 85% resistant to damage from magic, meaning they aren't as affected by enchantments and potions.

Wither Skeletons are the only mob that can drop their head when killed.

Zombies can break down wooden doors (on harder difficulty modes) and transform villagers into zombies.

Zombie Villagers can be transformed back into villagers under the right circumstances!

MINECRAFT'S SECRET MOBS

Did you know there are mobs that don't currently appear unless you summon them using the console? It's true, and if you're playing PC Version 1.9 (or later), here's how you can see them!

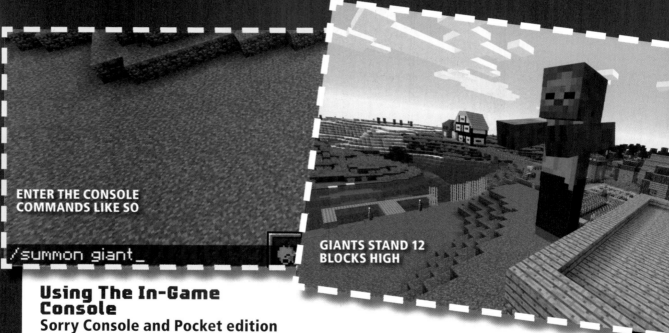

ENTER THE CONSOLE COMMANDS LIKE SO

/summon giant_

GIANTS STAND 12 BLOCKS HIGH

Using The In-Game Console

Sorry Console and Pocket edition players! The only way to summon these mobs is to use the in-game console on the PC edition. These mobs may come to your version later, so enjoy the sneak peek!

To access the in-game console, press / on the bottom right of the keyboard. Enter the summon commands given and the mob will appear next to you. For the commands to work, cheats must be enabled for the world you're playing in.

Giant Zombie

The giant zombie – aka the giant – is an oversized zombie six times as tall as a normal one. Unlike regular-sized zombies, there are no variant versions of the giant, so you can't get giant villager zombies or giant baby zombies.

To summon one, open the console and use the command:

/summon giant

Although giants have been in the game for some time, they never spawn on their own. They have no AI, so when summoned they'll stand still, facing south, and not move unless pushed or hit. The difficulty must be Easy or higher, otherwise the mob will disappear!

They can be killed, though! Giants have 100 hit points and drop five experience points, just like a normal zombie.

GIANT ZOMBIES ARE HUGE COMPARED TO NORMAL ONES

A ZOMBIE HORSE AND SKELETON HORSE

Zombie Horse

Although Minecraft 1.9 allows players to encounter the skeleton horse naturally, there's another variant of the horse – the zombie horse – that doesn't yet spawn unless forced to by the use of the console.

To summon a tame zombie horse, type the following command into the console:
/summon EntityHorse ~ ~ ~ {Type:4,Tame:1}
If you want the zombie to be neutral (unfriendly, but not aggressive), delete the comma and everything after it up until the second curly bracket.

Unfriendly zombie horses can't be tamed, so if you want to ride one you'll have to summon it tame already. They always have 15 health, can't ever breed and won't eat food! When killed, they drop rotten flesh instead of leather, and three experience.

Killer Bunny

Added at the same time as rabbits, the killer bunny is a hostile variant of rabbits that's in the game as a reference to a scene from *Monty Python and The Holy Grail*. It has all-white fur and horizontal red eyes. There are friendly white rabbits in the game, so don't get confused!

To summon a killer bunny, type:
/summon Rabbit ~ ~ ~ {RabbitType:99}
When spawned, they'll attack any player in a 16-block radius, moving quickly and jumping at them like a spider. They're immune to the Thorns enchantment, and won't despawn if the game is set to Peaceful!

The Killer Bunny

THE KILLER BUNNY HAS A NAME WHEN IT SPAWNS

THE KILLER BUNNY (LEFT) NEXT TO A NORMAL WHITE RABBIT (RIGHT)

VERSION-EXCLUSIVE SECRETS

If you play a version of Minecraft other than the PC edition, it can feel like you miss out on a lot of cool stuff. Luckily, the Pocket and Console Editions have some version-exclusive secrets!

BEETROOT STARTED LIFE IN POCKET EDITION

DYING TREES ARE COVERED IN VINES

Pocket Edition: Villages

In Pocket Edition, villages were more developed than other versions for a long time. If they intersected with water, their roads became wooden walkways, and it was even possible to find whole villages floating almost entirely on water. Instead of gravel paths, villages in temperate biomes generated grass paths – a feature that only came to Minecraft's PC Edition recently, in version 1.10.

Pocket Edition: Trees

The Pocket Edition has two alternate types of tree that aren't found in the normal one. The first, a "dying tree", looks like any normal tree except that its trunk is covered in vines. These form randomly, even from new saplings. The second is a "fallen tree", which is a log (sometimes covered in vines or mushrooms) lying on the ground near a stump. Neither of these appear in any edition other than Windows 10.

Pocket Edition: Huge Mushrooms

Although huge mushrooms appear in other versions, they can be taller in Pocket Edition (up to 13 blocks) and they generate naturally in swamps, which isn't true of other versions. The former will be incorporated into Minecraft 1.10, but it's not known whether the latter will!

YOU WON'T SEE
FALLEN TREES
ANYWHERE ELSE

SNOW LAYERS ON
POCKET EDITION
ARE UNEVEN

Pocket Edition: Cauldrons

Cauldrons in Pocket Edition can store things other than water, such as dye and potions. Witch huts that automatically generate have the chance of being filled with a random potion, which the player can collect in a glass bottle.

Pocket Edition: Snow

Just like in real life, snow doesn't fall in an even layer in Pocket Edition – instead, it builds up unevenly.

Pocket Edition: Jockeys

When baby zombies spawn, they have a small chance to be a jockey and will mount chickens, ocelots, wolves, other zombies, cows, pigs, sheep, spiders, and mooshrooms.

Console Edition: Nether Wart

In most versions, Nether wart appears only in limited amounts inside Nether fortresses. In Console Edition, it can grow almost anywhere in the Nether, as long as there's soul sand.

Console Edition: Minecarts

If you like building or riding rollercoasters, Console Edition is for you: minecarts go twice as fast compared to the PC edition!

Console Edition: Spawn Eggs

In Creative, it's possible to get spawn eggs for specific types of horses: there are separate spawn eggs for donkeys and mules.

Console Edition: Fireworks

Fireworks are available in most versions, but you have to craft them. In Console Edition, you can pick pre-crafted fireworks in Creative.

MINECARTS TRAVEL
FASTER IN THE
CONSOLE VERSION

CONSOLE EDITION
HAS SEPARATE
SPAWN EGGS FOR
DIFFERENT TYPES
OF HORSE

UNCRAFTABLE ITEMS

Minecraft is all about crafting, but not everything in the game can be crafted. Sometimes, you have to scavenge, trade, or even steal the items you need. Uncraftable items are super-rare, so here's our guide to how you get them and what you can do to hang onto them!

SADDLES CAN'T BE CRAFTED, SO THEY'RE QUITE VALUABLE

YOU CAN BUY SADDLES FROM A LEATHERWORKER

Saddles

If you want to ride a horse (mule, donkey or pig), you need a saddle. Unfortunately, saddles are precision pieces of craftwork that can't just be made by ANY player. There are several ways to get a saddle: you can find one in a chest (they appear in stronghold altars, Nether fortress chests, desert and jungle temples, dungeons, End cities and village blacksmiths – almost all of them!) and you can trade with a leatherworker villager. They cost 8-10 emeralds and are a third-tier trade.

If you're feeling sneaky, you can also kill a saddled pig or steal one off a saddled horse in a multiplayer game, but that's not very nice! Luckily, saddles don't break, so once you've got one there isn't much need for another!

Enchanted Golden Apples

Previously craftable, the enchanted golden apple is no longer available except in chests. Previously, it could be made by surrounding a normal apple with blocks of gold, the same way a golden apple can be made by surrounding an apple with gold ingots. It also used to be possible to collect an enchanted golden apple by killing Notch in a multiplayer game (which is why they used to be known informally as "notch apples"), but this is no longer the case.

ENCHANTED
GOLDEN APPLES
GLOW PURPLE

DRAGON
HEADS
SPAWN ON
END SHIPS

Mob Heads

There are six different mob heads, none of which can be crafted. You can find a guide to collecting all six later on in the How To section!

Music Discs

There are 12 music discs, all of which you can play in a jukebox. None of the discs are craftable, but you can find two, 'Cat' and '13', in dungeon chests. The remaining 10 are dropped whenever a skeleton's arrow kills a creeper. On the Console Edition, you can find all of the music discs within chests hidden in the tutorial world.

MAKE A SKELETON
KILL A CREEPER TO
GET A MUSIC DISC

Horse Armour

There are three types of horse armour: iron, gold and diamond. Unlike other types of armour, gold is stronger than iron, though diamond remains the strongest. You can only find horse armour in chests (check the Treasure Guide section for full details), but once you collect it, it never takes damage so you can keep using it until your horse dies.

Name Tags

You can use a name tag to give any mob (including villagers) a name by renaming them on an anvil. Name tags can be found as treasure from fishing, or in dungeon and abandoned mineshaft chests. You can only use them once, but once you name a mob it will stay in your world with its name until it dies.

Thunderclops

ONCE YOU
USE A NAME
TAG, IT'S
GONE, SO
MAKE IT
COUNT!

127

EXPERT HOW TO GUIDES

How To Bonanza!

We're nearly at the end now, so let's give you specific advice on how to do some of the trickiest things in Minecraft! How do you cure zombies? How do you summon the ender dragon? How can you make fancy fireworks? And how can you defeat the toughest enemies that Minecraft has to offer? This, the final chapter of our guide, has all the answers waiting for you. Good luck, adventurer!

HOW TO DEFEAT THE
ENDER DRAGON

THE ENDER DRAGON IS POWERFUL

IT WILL HOVER OVER THE PORTAL FRAME, SO HURT IT THERE

EVENTUALLY YOU'LL DEFEAT THE DRAGON

YOU'LL GET LOADS OF EXPERIENCE!

The ender dragon is the first boss mob you'll face in Minecraft and maybe the hardest, though not as scary as the wither!

You'll face the dragon when you arrive in the End and immediately have to fight it, so get everything you need before you enter the End portal in a stronghold. We recommend strong armour with defence enchantments, an Infinity-enchanted bow, and plenty of healing potions and food!

The first step in killing the dragon is to use a bow and arrow to destroy the ender crystals found on top of the tall obsidian pillars dotted around the End. When the dragon gets close to them, they heal its health, so there's no point trying to kill it until they've been taken out.

Some of the pillars have protective irons bars that you need to climb up and break, but don't hit the ender crystals as they'll explode in your face!

After they've all been destroyed, stay near the portal frame. The dragon will swoop down periodically, so dodge its attacks, heal yourself with potions or golden apples, and chip away at its health! It isn't affected by negative status effects like poison, so save your fancier weapons for fending off any angry endermen nearby.

When the dragon is killed, you'll collect 12,000 experience points and gain access to the activated End portal, which takes you to your spawn point in the Overworld!

HOW TO SUMMON THE ENDER DRAGON AGAIN

If you've killed the ender dragon once but fancy another tough fight, you can summon and fight it as many times as you like. Here's how to bring that deadliest of beasts back from the dead!

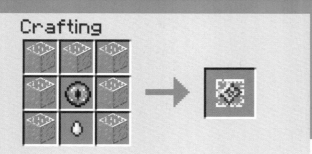

Crafting

Ingredients

To summon the ender dragon, you need four ender crystals. You can craft one using the following ingredients:
- 7 x glass blocks
- 1 x eye of ender
- 1 x ghast tear

Instructions

Summoning an ender dragon is a good idea for a lot of reasons. If you're trying to craft lingering potions, it will give you the opportunity to collect extra dragon's breath. If you're low on experience, you can get 500 points every time you kill the dragon again (the first time you get 12,000 points, but unfortunately that's reduced for every extra dragon you kill).

To summon a dragon, place the four ender crystals on each side of the End portal. This will cause the portal to turn into End stone, regenerate the ender crystals on the top of the obsidian pillars found around the central island, and thus release a new dragon.

As before, the only way to leave the End is to either die or kill the dragon so that you can access the End portal again. Don't summon a dragon unless you're prepared to go down fighting it – and remember to bring glass bottles. You don't want to miss that dragon's breath at the end!

ENDER CRYSTALS ARE WHAT HEAL A DRAGON

THE END PORTAL ACTIVATES WHEN THE DRAGON IS SLAIN

PUT FOUR ENDER CRYSTALS ON THE PORTAL FRAME TO RESURRECT THE DRAGON

131

HOW TO SUMMON THE WITHER

THIS PAINTING IS A CLUE TO WHAT YOU SHOULD DO

BUILD THIS FROM SOUL SAND AND WITHER SKULLS

IT'S ALMOST HERE...

WATCH OUT FOR ITS EXPLOSIVE ENTRANCE

To fight the wither, you must first create it, similar to building a golem. To do this, place four blocks of soul sand in a "T" shape, with three wither skeleton heads on the top row. Both of these items are only found in the Nether, but you can summon the wither anywhere.

Soul sand is easy to find in the Nether, but the wither skeleton heads can only be found by killing large numbers of wither skeletons, which are only found in Nether fortresses. You normally need to kill around 120 wither skeletons to get three wither skeleton heads, but carrying a sword with a Looting enchantment can lower the average to around 40.

When the wither awakens, it will cause a big explosion that damages anything close by, so get out of the way once the third head is placed!

When active, the wither is hostile to all mobs except zombies and skeletons. Its wither skull attack causes explosions and poisons mobs, and it breaks any block it comes into contact with other than End portal frames and bedrock.

Once you've summoned the wither, you then have to fight it. Killing the wither causes it to drop a Nether star, which you can use to create beacons. You can summon and kill the wither as many times as you like, but once is usually enough!

HOW TO DEFEAT
THE WITHER

From the moment it spawns, the wither is hostile! If you succeed in killing this fearsome beast, enjoy it – nothing in Minecraft is harder than this!

When the wither notices a mob or player, it attacks with its wither skulls. The blasts move slowly and explode on impact, and on Normal/Hard difficulty curse their targets with the Wither (Level II) effect.

This is similar to poison and injures the player over time, but turns the health bar black and can kill you!

Each of the wither's heads can fire skulls at a different target. If it comes into contact with blocks, they're destroyed in seconds. Only bedrock and End portal frames are immune!

You can only see the wither's health bar when you're looking at it. If left alone, it will regenerate health by half a heart every second. Golems and tame wolves can distract the wither from you, but can rarely get close enough to attack it, and the wither can steal their health.

When the wither reaches half of its health, it will gain the Wither Armour effect, which makes it immune to arrows and potions. Luckily, it also stops flying very high, and can be attacked with swords.

The best way to fight the wither is to use a diamond sword enchanted with Smite (Level V) and a bow enchanted with Power (Level V) and Infinity. Protect yourself by eating golden apples and wearing Diamond Armour with Protection (Level IV).

THE WITHER WILL ATTACK ANYTHING

YOU'LL HAVE TO GET CLOSE!

TRAPPING IT IN A TUNNEL CAN HELP

WHEN YOU'RE CLOSE TO KILLING IT, THE WITHER SPAWNS ARMOUR

133

HOW TO CURE A ZOMBIE VILLAGER

You spend a lot of time killing mobs, but if you're willing to put in the effort you can feed some good back into the Overworld by giving a zombie villager a new chance at a normal life!

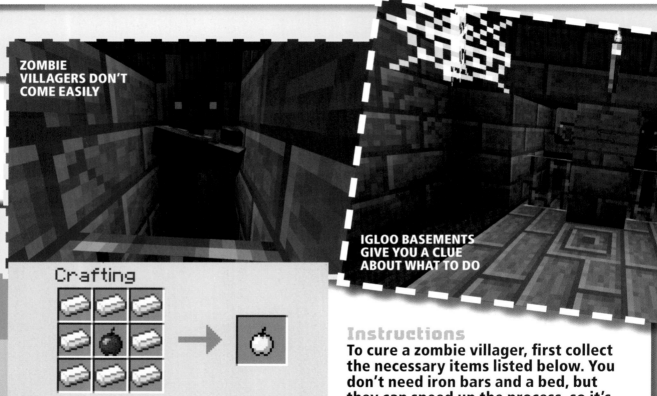

ZOMBIE VILLAGERS DON'T COME EASILY

IGLOO BASEMENTS GIVE YOU A CLUE ABOUT WHAT TO DO

Crafting

What You Need

Curing a zombie villager means getting hold of a few things:

1 x golden apple
(1 x apple, 8 x gold ingots)
1 x Splash Potion of Weakness
(brew a fermented spider eye and gunpowder into a water bottle)
Optional: iron bars
(6 x iron ingots)
Optional: bed
(3 x wool + 3 x wood planks)

Instructions

To cure a zombie villager, first collect the necessary items listed below. You don't need iron bars and a bed, but they can speed up the process, so it's worth getting them if possible!

Once you have the necessary items, you need to find a zombie villager. These are easy to spot – they look like zombies, but have the large head and nose typical of a regular villager. Before you try to cure the zombie, it's worth trapping it somewhere.

This is where the bed and iron bars come in, because placing those items near a zombie villager will make the healing process happen faster. If you build a "jail cell", you can use a lead or fishing rod to take a zombie villager to it, although you can just trap them wherever you find them if you don't mind waiting.

GOLDEN APPLES APPEAR IN CHESTS

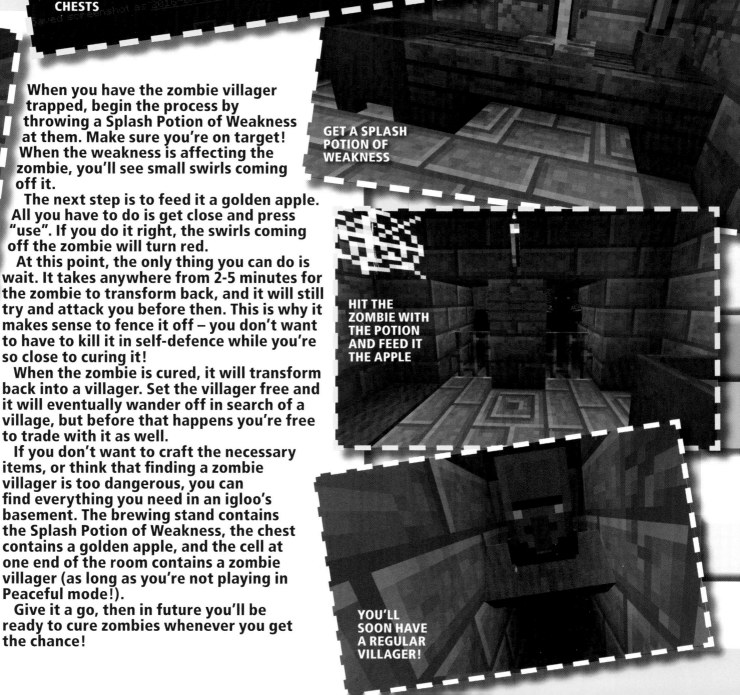

GET A SPLASH POTION OF WEAKNESS

When you have the zombie villager trapped, begin the process by throwing a Splash Potion of Weakness at them. Make sure you're on target! When the weakness is affecting the zombie, you'll see small swirls coming off it.

The next step is to feed it a golden apple. All you have to do is get close and press "use". If you do it right, the swirls coming off the zombie will turn red.

At this point, the only thing you can do is wait. It takes anywhere from 2-5 minutes for the zombie to transform back, and it will still try and attack you before then. This is why it makes sense to fence it off – you don't want to have to kill it in self-defence while you're so close to curing it!

When the zombie is cured, it will transform back into a villager. Set the villager free and it will eventually wander off in search of a village, but before that happens you're free to trade with it as well.

If you don't want to craft the necessary items, or think that finding a zombie villager is too dangerous, you can find everything you need in an igloo's basement. The brewing stand contains the Splash Potion of Weakness, the chest contains a golden apple, and the cell at one end of the room contains a zombie villager (as long as you're not playing in Peaceful mode!).

Give it a go, then in future you'll be ready to cure zombies whenever you get the chance!

HIT THE ZOMBIE WITH THE POTION AND FEED IT THE APPLE

YOU'LL SOON HAVE A REGULAR VILLAGER!

HOW TO WRITE A BOOK

KILL SQUID TO GET INK SACS

GET BOOKS FROM LIBRARIES

Crafting

Page 1 of 1

Write whatever you like here!_

Sign   Done

START WRITING!

Sometimes it's useful to keep notes when you play Minecraft. Rather than use a notepad, why not write them in-game using a book? That way, you'll never lose your notes and you can even pass them on to other players!

Ingredients
A book (3 x paper + 6 x leather)
A feather
An ink sac

Construction
Craft together a book with a feather and an ink sac, and you'll create a book & quill. These are books that can be written in. You can write as much or as little as you like, and when you "sign" the book its content will become fixed as a written book.

Behaviour
Written books can be read or copied using additional book & quills on a crafting table. When a book is signed, it will display the name of the player who wrote it. You also have the chance to choose a title of up to 16 characters long.

However, it's often more useful to leave a book "unsigned" so you can keep editing its contents, writing notes, reminders and useful information down.

Books can have up to 50 pages with 256 characters per page. When you're editing a book in single-player mode, the world will freeze. It's possible to use copy and paste to enter text into books, as long as the text is shorter than a single page.

136

HOW TO CREATE AN ENDER CHEST

Ender chests are hard to make but highly useful! They contain a storage area that can be accessed from any ender chest, so are great for transporting rare items without the danger of carrying them.

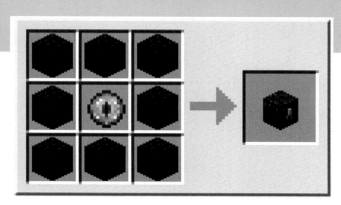

Ingredients
You'll need the following items:
1 x eye of ender
8 x obsidian

Construction
To build an ender chest, all you need to do is surround one eye of ender with eight blocks of obsidian. But remember – for the chest to be of any use, you have to make at least two! Eyes of ender are created by combining 1 x blaze powder and 1 x ender pearl.

Behaviour
Ender chests contain 27 storage slots, which can be used to store items in a single accessible area. If you carry an ender chest with you while exploring and leave one in your base, you can easily get access to backup tools and armour, or use it to share items across large distances in the game.

Note that ender chest inventories can't be shared by different players – each player has their own version of the storage area that they can access. This does mean that in multiplayer one chest can be used by lots of different people and will contain different items for each player.

Ender chests can't be mined unless you use a Silk Touch pickaxe. Normally they break when they're mined, dropping eight blocks of obsidian in the process.

You can sometimes find ender chests in End cities.

AN ENDER CHEST CAN'T BE LOOTED

MAKE MORE THAN ONE AND YOU CAN ACCESS THE STUFF IN IT ANYWHERE

YOU CAN COLLECT ENDER CHESTS FROM END CITIES

137

HOW TO CRAFT A SHIELD

Shields are one of the latest additions to Minecraft and allow you to defend yourself from attacks of all kinds, as well as display your allegiance to a particular guild or faction!

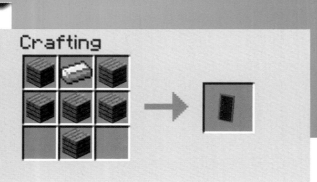

Crafting

SHIELD PROTECT YOU IN A FIGHT

YOU CAN EVEN HOLD TWO!

CRAFT A BANNER WITH A SHIELD

Shields can be held in the main or offhand slot. They can be used as well as or instead of a weapon!

Ingredients

6 x wood planks (any type)
An iron ingot
To add a pattern to your shield, craft it together with a banner (optional)

Construction

To craft a shield, simply place items on a crafting grid in the pattern shown. The items are all quite common so you should be able to get a shield quite early in the game if you want one! If you wish to apply a pattern to your shield, you only have to craft the completed shield with a banner to apply its effect.

Behaviour

When using the shield, you can hold it in either of your hands to defend yourself from attacks by other mobs and players. Holding a shield in one of your hands makes you walk slowly – as slow as if you were sneaking – but if the shield is in your inventory you'll be able to walk at a normal speed.

Take care when using one – if the shield is hit by an axe, it can be temporarily disabled, and if the shield is hit by an arrow, the arrow will bounce off and hurt any nearby mobs or players that it hits!

HOW TO CRAFT A BANNER

Banners are decorative flags that you can hang around your world to show territory and ownership, or just make the place look cool! They can hang on walls or be planted in the ground, and even added to shields to decorate them.

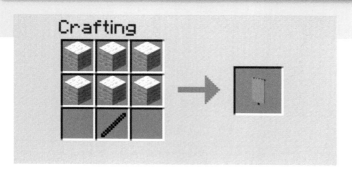

Crafting

A BANNER IN THE OVERWORLD

A GREEN BRICK BANNER

BANNERS CAN SHOW YOUR ALLEGIANCE

Ingredients
- 6 x wool (any colour, but must all be the same colour)
- A stick

To add a pattern to a banner, craft it with:
- Dye (any colour, any amount)
- 1 x vines
- 1 x bricks
- 1 x creeper/wither skull head
- 1 x oxeye daisy
- 1 x enchanted golden apple

Construction
When you dye a banner, the shape and placement of dye on the crafting grid creates different patterns, so don't be afraid to experiment! Putting three dye in a diagonal will create a diagonal line across the banner, for instance. There are loads of combinations! If you put the dye in a "Y" shape, it will create a gradient.

You can craft six items with banners to create patterns:

- Vines create a wavy border around the banner
- Bricks create a brick-textured background
- Creeper heads create a creeper face logo
- Wither skulls add a skull and crossbones
- Oxeye daisies add a flower logo
- Enchanted golden apples add a Mojang logo

Behaviour
Banners can be crafted with dye or pattern blocks up to six times to overlay different patterns or shapes on top of one another, and you can wash one layer off at a time using a cauldron. Once you have a pattern you like, you can copy an existing banner by crafting it with a blank one.

139

HOW TO MAKE
FIREWORKS

They serve almost no practical purpose, but fireworks are great fun! To create a basic firework, you need to create a firework star then put it in a rocket. Here's how you get to that point.

Crafting

A SIMPLE FIREWORK

Crafting → Firework Rocket
Flight Duration: 3
Star-shaped
Green
Inventory

Ingredients

The most important ingredient in a firework is a craftable item called a firework star. To make it, you'll require:
- 1 x gunpowder
- 1 x any colour dye

To make the firework explode, you must place it in a rocket. To create the firework rocket, you need:
- 1 x paper (3 x sugar cane)
- Up to 3 x gunpowder
- One or more firework stars

Construction

First, you must build a firework star by crafting together the ingredients. You can customise firework stars further by adding extra items into the mixture (check over the page for more details!).

When the firework star is complete, craft it with the paper and gunpowder to make a rocket. You can add up to three pieces of gunpowder to a rocket, and the more gunpowder you add, the

further the rocket will travel. You can also use up to seven firework stars in one rocket, which will explode simultaneously.

Behaviour

You can place rockets on the ground or in a dispenser. When lit, a firework will shoot upwards (even if launched from a dispenser) and explode.

Firework rockets are one of the few items that can fly outside of the normal world limits and explode at heights above 256 blocks. Firework explosions don't damage players or mobs.

FIREWORKS LAUNCH INSTANTLY WHEN PLACED

SEVERAL FIREWORKS

HOW TO CUSTOMISE
FIREWORKS

Basic fireworks are pretty, but they're a lot more fun if you customise them. There are thousands to create and some are quite complex to build, so here's our guide to making them!

Ingredients

1 x firework star
One or more of the following: fire charge, gold nugget, feather, glowstone dust, mob head or diamond

Construction

Crafting items with firework stars can alter the colour, shape and effect of the eventual firework. You don't have to add all of the ingredients when the firework star is first made, as crafting a compatible item with a firework star creates another firework star with the altered effect. Some items exclude other ones – for instance, you can't add two shape items to a firework, or double up on a single item.

Behaviour

There are two effect items you can add to firework stars: a diamond will cause trails on the particles, and glowstone dust will make the particles twinkle. You can add both to one firework star if you want! There are four shape ingredients you can add, but firework stars can only contain one. By default, the firework shape is "small ball". Adding a

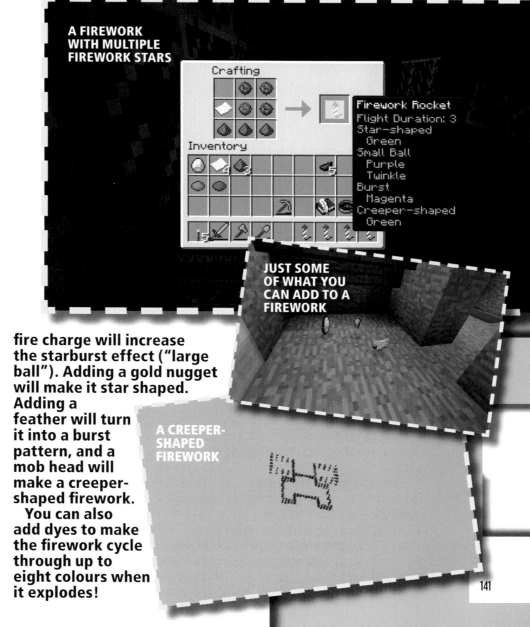

A FIREWORK WITH MULTIPLE FIREWORK STARS

JUST SOME OF WHAT YOU CAN ADD TO A FIREWORK

A CREEPER-SHAPED FIREWORK

fire charge will increase the starburst effect ("large ball"). Adding a gold nugget will make it star shaped. Adding a feather will turn it into a burst pattern, and a mob head will make a creeper-shaped firework.

You can also add dyes to make the firework cycle through up to eight colours when it explodes!

HOW TO MAKE A BEACON

DEFEAT THE WITHER AND COLLECT A NETHER STAR

BUILD A ONE-, TWO-, THREE- OR FOUR-LEVEL BEACON

USE STAINED GLASS TO CHANGE THE BEAM'S COLOUR

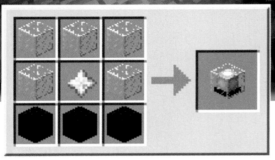

Beacons have two purposes: as a navigation aid and to power up nearby players. They're very hard to build, but if you want the challenge, here's how you can try.

Ingredients
At least 9 x iron/gold/emerald/ diamond blocks (81 ingots or gems in total)
A beacon block (3 x obsidian, 1 x Nether star, 5 x glass blocks)

Construction
To build a beacon, you must construct at least a 3x3 platform of metal or mineral blocks then place a beacon block on the centre. This is a one-level pyramid. The biggest and strongest beacons have four levels, which requires 164 mineral blocks, or 1,476 gems/ingots!

Beacons must be under open sky to activate correctly. You don't have to use the same type of blocks to build a pyramid, and the material has no effect on the beacon's behaviour – only its appearance – so it's probably easiest to use iron blocks!

Behaviour
Once lit, a beacon will fire a beam of light into the sky, which is visible from up to 170 blocks away. You can use stained glass blocks or stained glass panes to change the colour of the light. In all editions other than Pocket Edition, you'll receive an achievement for creating a full beacon.

HOW TO CHARGE A BEACON

Once a beacon has been built, you have to charge it to activate its particular status effect, which will last for 11 seconds on a one-level pyramid, 13 seconds on a two-level pyramid, 15 seconds on a three-level pyramid and 17 seconds on a four-level pyramid. Here's how!

You have to feed or charge a beacon so that the players within range will receive their status effects. You can use any of four items to charge the beacon: iron ingots, gold ingots, emerald ingots or diamonds. The item you choose has no effect on the power a beacon provides.

When the beacon is charged, you can select one of the five primary powers and potentially a secondary power (depending on how large it is):

Single-Level Pyramids and above

Speed (Level I) – Increases movement speed
Haste (Level I) – Increases mining speed

Two-Level Pyramids and above

Resistance (Level I) – Decreases all incoming damage
Jump Boost (Level I) – Increases jumping height and distance

Three-Level Pyramids and above

Strength (Level I) – Increases melee damage

Four-Level Pyramids

On a four-level pyramid, you can also activate the secondary power, which increases the primary power to Level II and adds Regeneration (Level I), which makes player health recover.

Changing Power

When you activate a power, the item you used to charge the beacon will be immediately consumed. The beacon doesn't need to be fed more to keep the power active, but if you want to change the power at a future point you must feed the beacon with more resources to do so!

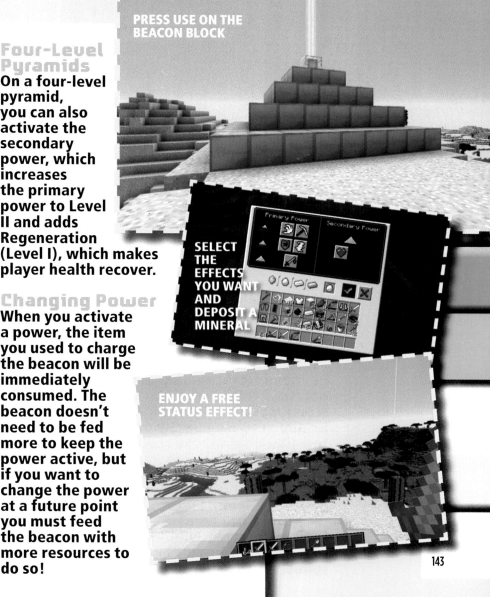

PRESS USE ON THE BEACON BLOCK

SELECT THE EFFECTS YOU WANT AND DEPOSIT A MINERAL

ENJOY A FREE STATUS EFFECT!

HOW TO COLLECT
MOB HEADS

Mob heads are quite rare drops that you can miss out on completely if you're not actively trying to get them. You can place them as blocks or wear them as helmets to scare your friends – some even have special uses! But where do you find them and how can you get them? Here's our guide to finding all six of these rare items.

YOU NEED A CHARGED CREEPER TO GET SKELETON, CREEPER AND ZOMBIE HEADS

Skeleton Skull, Creeper Head & Zombie Head

These three types of head can only be obtained if the corresponding mob is killed in an explosion caused by a charged creeper. Charged creepers are themselves quite rare, but their explosions are large, so it isn't hard to get them to kill another mob once they appear. Remember, if you use a flint & steel, you can force them to detonate immediately, so you can lure mobs to them then set off the creeper!

When worn, skeleton, creeper and zombie heads will reduce the detection range for the corresponding mob by 50%. This works on top of range reductions from other sources, such as sneaking or invisibility, so mob heads are great for avoiding common mobs.

Wither Skeleton Skull

Wither skeleton skulls can be collected by killing wither skeletons, with each kill by a player or tame wolf having a 2.5% charge of dropping a wither skull. This means you have to kill around 40 skeletons to collect one skull, although the actual number can be a lot higher or lower!

Wither skeleton skulls are used to summon the wither and don't affect the detection range for wither skeletons if worn.

Dragon Head

These are the only type of mob head to generate naturally, and do so on End ships in the End. This means you won't be able to get one (without cheating!) until you've played through a lot of the game and defeated the ender dragon.

A HEAD TO COLLECT! LUCKY

WITHER SKELETONS DROP SKULLS – EVENTUALLY

Although they only spawn occasionally (End cities are rare, and End ships don't appear in every End city), the End is infinite, so there's an infinite number of dragon heads in the game. Be prepared to do a LOT of exploring, though!

Dragon heads can be made to animate (with their mouths opening and closing) if attached to a redstone charge. They're also longer and larger than the other mob heads in the game, but can still be worn as a mask!

Player Head

The player head is impossible to collect normally, but can be acquired in Creative mode or through the use of the in-game console (on the PC edition only). It can take the skin of any specified player, but by default it will appear as the head of your current skin.

Mob Head Secrets

Creeper heads can be added to banners to create a creeper face pattern on them in black (if used alone) or any colour (if crafted with a dye).

Wither skeleton skulls can be added to banners to create a skull and crossbones pattern on them in black (if used alone) or any other colour (if crafted with a dye).

You can also add ANY mob head to a firework star to make it explode in the shape of a creeper face.

A DRAGON HEAD ON AN END SHIP

YOU CAN'T GET THE PLAYER HEAD WITHOUT USING CREATIVE MODE

WEAR A CREEPER HEAD TO STOP THEM ATTACKING YOU

145

Published by Dennis Lifestyle Ltd. 30 Cleveland St,
London W1T 4JD. Company registered in England.

Editorial:
James Hunt, with Simon Brew and John Moore
Production Editor: Rachel Storry
Production: Stephen Catherall

Publisher Dharmesh Mistry
Group MD Ian Westwood
Operations Director Robin Ryan
MD of Advertising Julian Lloyd-Evans
Newstrade Director David Barker
Chief Operating Officer Brett Reynolds
Group Finance Director Ian Leggett
Chief Executive James Tye
Company Founder Felix Dennis

PRINT Southern Print
DISTRIBUTION Seymour Distribution

LICENSING & SYNDICATION
To license this product please contact
Carlotta Serantoni: +44 (0) 20 79076550
Email: **carlotta_serantoni@dennis.co.uk**
To syndicate content from this product please contact
Anj Halai: +44(0) 20 7907 6132
Email: **Anj_Halai@dennis.co.uk**

DISCLAIMER
Minecraft is a registered trademark of Mojang Synergies
AB ("Mojang"). The screenshots and artwork shown
in this publication were taken from Minecraft, a game
published by Mojang, and from Microsoft XBOX websites.
Game design, programming and graphics for Minecraft
were authored by Notch (Markus Persson), officers,
employees and/or freelancers of Mojang. This is a 100%
unofficial and independent publication which is in no
way licensed, authorised or endorsed by or otherwise
connected in any way with Mojang or any other
individuals who are authors of Minecraft.

Names, brands and logos mentioned in this publication
may be protected by trade mark or other intellectual
property rights of one or several legal jurisdictions. Any
reference to such marks in no way implies that they are
not protected under applicable law, nor is it implied that
there is any commercial or other relationship between the
publisher and that trademark holder.

The publisher excludes all liability for the content
and services provided by any websites or other third
party publications or games reviewed and shall not be
responsible for and does not endorse any advertising,
products or resources including those available from any
third party external resources including websites and
we shall not be liable to any party for any information,
services or resources made available through them.

All copyrights recognised and used specifically for the
purpose of criticism and review.

LIABILITY
While every care was taken during the production of this
MagBook, the publishers cannot be held responsible for any
errors or omissions in it. The paper used within this MagBook
is produced from sustainable fibre and are manufactured by
mills with a valid chain of custody.

Projects and images are the work of their original creators.
All rights acknowledged.